THE AU

From a very young age, Marian Matthews felt and saw things that made her question everything she had been taught about the nature of reality. This book charts the journey of her search for the truth about the mystery of human consciousness and the ultimate nature of the reality in which we live, and in so doing uncovers some vital universal truths.

Not an 'ivory tower' academic, her background is that of wife, mother, grandmother, thinker, student, teacher, charity worker and politician. She has always had an interest in philosophy and the science of the nature of the universe as well as spiritual matters.

Follow her on this journey of exploration and you will never look at things in the same way again.

To view all of our titles please go to:

transpersonalbooks.com

Aspects of Reality

A User's Guide to the Universe

Aspects of Reality

A User's Guide to the Universe

Marian Matthews

Cover design by
Ian Thorp

Talking

Whoever holds the talking
stick has within their
hands the sacred
power of words –
only the one
who holds the
stick may
speak

but
must
speak the
truth about
personal
understanding
and experience

Stick

First published in Great Britain by
Talking Stick
an imprint of Archive Publishing
Wimborne Dorset BH21 1HB England
01202 848352

www.marianmatthews.com

A CIP Record for this book is available from
The British Cataloguing in Publication data office.

ISBN 978 1 906289 21 8 (Paperback)

Printed and bound by
Melita Press, Malta.

ACKNOWLEDGEMENTS

Thanks to all my beloved children and grandchildren and to the countless other friends and colleagues, particularly Chloe, Sam, Emma, Barbara, Joy, Marian and Jean, who have supported me and provided me with much inspiration.

Particular thanks to my son Mark Holland who has been a very hard task master, and to my patient husband Toby without whose love and care the work would not have been completed.

And finally, thanks to Ian Thorp of Talking Stick for his help and encouragement in bringing this book to fruition.

www.marianmatthews.com

CONTENTS

PREFACE

Who are we? Where do we come from? Why are we here? What is the true nature of this reality that we find ourselves living in? Does society actually know the truth about our origins, and the creation of the universe? These are just some of the questions that have occupied so many minds, over so many thousands of years. Many people do just accept what society or religion tell them about the way things are, where we came from and what we are doing here on earth. Others are just not interested in the bigger picture, as they live their lives in the here and now. As questioning human beings, however, the curious among us do feel the need to know more.

There have always been those who have questioned what they have been taught about reality in our culture. In previous times they have often been punished for it. They have queried the truth about the underlying nature of ourselves, the universe and all that is in it. From a very young age, I have been doing the same. Along with many others, I gradually began to glimpse the anomalies in the world around me. I began to see the contradictions in the notions of reality that I had been brought up with.

The aim of this book is to explain, and pass on to you, all the wisdom and insights that I have learnt or come to understand over the years. I have thought long and hard about the conundrum that is life. I have always seen things that did not fit with the way I had been taught they were, and tried to make sense of them. What is the truth about the reality that we find ourselves living in? Is what we see all there is? These are the questions that not enough people ask.

It is a useful analogy to compare reality to one of those multi-faceted glitter balls that are sometimes found on night club ceilings. They are as they are, but as they turn and turn and have the lights shine on them, all an individual can see are the reflections of light bouncing back. Not only that, but the reflections look slightly different to everyone observing, depending where they are standing under the ball, and what light is shinning on each facet. This is the position with reality; all we can do is to try and look beyond the reflections we can see, to the ultimate truth beyond.

What follows is an attempt to put in a logical framework the acquired knowledge and insights into the hidden truths of our lives. It is an attempt to point out the conundrums that abound in our systems, and how these can impact on our understanding of the way that the universe works around us. It is also an attempt to throw light on possible new and different realities from those currently accepted by mainstream thinkers. Understanding of these can enable us to live better lives.

There are clues there, reflections of aspects of reality, almost in plain sight that are finally, to me anyway, beginning to make coherent sense and reveal a stunning alternative big picture. It is also a very personal journey, using both my own experience, and that of others, as well as whatever science and other research is appropriate.

In my research I looked both at the basic science of who we are, and all the exceptions and anomalies which indicated that what we were taught by society was not, and could not be, the whole story. To this end I delved into biology, cosmology, philosophy, the nature of human consciousness, high science, ghosts, spirits, communication with the dead, prediction of the future, healing and even the possibilities of aliens. I finished with my seven identified reflections of reality, and how we can use these to improve and enhance our lives.

This is not a textbook or an academic treatise. I am not a scientist or an ivory tower academic. I am just an ordinary, curious, thinking person. The science, explained where necessary, is that which seems to be the consensus of current scientific thinking at the time of writing. Details may change but the fundamental principles usually remain constant. Interestingly enough, it is in the high science that some of the most interesting anomalies, which question the nature of reality, occur. In writing, I found that there is more variation in the understanding of the true nature of reality in our society than one would assume, or expect, on first looking at the subject.

Please join me on this exciting journey. For many years, it has been as if I have been doing a gigantic jigsaw puzzle in my head. I felt, even from a small child, that the reality that we were taught, by church, school and society, was not necessarily the complete picture of how things were. This, I feel, has turned out to be the case. Returning to first principles, I have been putting together a design of reality without being aware of the final picture. I have just matched the pieces that seem to fit together perfectly. Some straight lines have appeared, and some linkages are becoming logical. But the puzzle is not yet complete; perhaps you can help me finish it.

It may be that, as limited creatures, we can never know the complete answers. Maybe we are not supposed to know the true nature of our reality. All we can hope for are glimpses, reflections, and insights into the way things, and humanity, actually are.

Marian Matthews
Blandford Forum
April 2012

CHAPTER ONE

Who do we think we are anyway?

How to begin – that is the difficult bit. The problem is how to put into words my understanding and insights into the true nature of the reality we find ourselves living in. I have thought long and hard about the conundrum that is life. As many people do, I have always seen things that did not fit with the way that I had been taught reality was, and tried to make sense of them. The intention is to pass to you, the reader, all the insights into the true nature of reality that I have acquired over time. The aim is to paint a compelling alternative big picture of our universe to that which we have grown up with.

What is the truth about the reality that we find ourselves living in? Are things how we have been taught they were? What could the big picture of life, the universe and everything actually be? These are questions that not enough people ask, but ones I will try to answer, or at least give some useful clues to, in the following chapters.

In any search for knowledge or clarification of facts, it is important to start with what we think we know for sure. This is never truer than in our search for the truth about the absolute nature of our reality. The first questions I asked myself, then, concerned ourselves. What do we know about us for sure? Who actually are the human race, when it comes down to it? All we can be certain of is that we are some sort of living beings, existing on a relatively small planet. We have organized ourselves into some sort of co-operative society. But who actually are these living beings? Where did they come from, and what are they doing here? What do they actually know, for sure, about themselves and their place in the universe?

Who are we and where do we come from?

The answer is, of course, that we believe ourselves to be members of the so-called human race. We do appear to live on a smallish home planet, which we call earth. This earth is part of a solar system of nine planets circling a medium-sized star, our sun. It seems to be the only inhabited planet in this star, or solar, system. Our solar system is itself part of a vast, mostly unexplored greater universe of stars. We are part of a much bigger picture. Scientists have not yet found the limits, the end of this universe. Stronger and stronger telescopes have revealed that even seemingly empty patches of the night sky are filled with more galaxies and stars, without visible end.

We manage to live on our home planet and thrive because the power of our sun drives a biosphere that supports human, and all animal and plant life. We are part of this harmonious system. Biologists tell us that we are just one member of a complex evolutionary tree of plants and animals. We are classified as Homo Sapiens, man apes, top of planet earth's animal evolutionary tree. We are supposed to be the most evolved of many diverse animals that inhabit the earth.

The human journey

From our own observations, we know that on this earth, as Homo Sapiens, we are born, we live our lives, and we die. There are two sexes of human being, with slightly different reproductive equipment, called male and female. The biological mechanism by which we are conceived and born involves a man and a woman making love. A male sperm fertilizes a female egg to create an embryo. This grows in the female womb, and nine or so months later a baby human being is born. In this way the human race reproduces itself and continues.

We observe other human beings living around and with us. We see babies growing up to be adults and living complex lives, interacting with each other. We age, sometimes sicken, and die and are mourned by our loved ones. People generally accept that physical death happens and is inevitable.

Our life on earth can be seen as a journey. It is a seemingly natural progression. From cradle to grave we exist on this world. We are born, we grow up, we make decisions and live the best life we can. Things and events seem to happen to us either by our own choice or by outside intervention. We mature and learn and hopefully pass on our genes and our wisdom. Eventually we die, or pass on, or pass over into an unknown afterlife.

What is being human?

We are taught to be human by those around us. It is interesting that we are seemingly born with just the instincts that we need to survive, but no knowledge. As babies we are seemingly blank slates. We are brought up by parents who are part of society and teach us both how to look after ourselves physically, and also what society expects us to know and understand. We become human by education and instinct.

We do observe and make our own judgments about how things are and what to do, to some extent. But that which we observe is usually coloured by the sort of things that we learn from our parents or peers. From the time we start school, and beyond, we are taught what society considers appropriate. We are schooled to fit in and take best advantage of this society. We are not taught to look beyond the accepted way of looking at the world, or to question accepted fundamentals. We almost never question the logic of how society is actually organized or who we, as beings, actually are. Indeed such questions are sometimes seen as dangerous. In some societies you can be severely punished for even having questioning thoughts on such topics. I very quickly learnt not to question things as a child even if they did not seem right at the time. It was simply not done.

To get back to basics though, we must first look at what we actually are. What makes us human? We know that we have a brain, which both controls and regulates our physical body. This brain is said to generate a mind. Our minds develop individuality and personality, they also observe the world and make decisions. We develop differently, depending on our genetics, education, experiences and upbringing. We have emotions and feelings and hearts, and some would say souls. We understand that we are organic, biodegradable beings. We are born, we live and we die and degrade. As we look around us we see fellow humans of all ages, shapes and sizes. We interact with others in the complex political and economic system we call society. We are conscious, thinking beings and aware that we are alive.

We also become human, rather than animal, in our understanding of what happens after physical death. Although we can be physically seen to be born, and understand that it is a consequence of a physical process, what actually happens when we die is a matter for much debate. It is at the end of the physical life process that there arise many interesting theories concerning what happens next. It is at this point that some interesting reflections of reality begin to show themselves. Although we are one species, different cultures and religions have different ideas on what happens when the physical body fails.

Some people feel that we go on after death. Others feel we just die and cease to exist. Some believe we live many times to experience and improve our souls by our own choice. Others just do not look much beyond what we are taught about the process by the church, state and our school teachers. There are thus many variations on the theories about what it actually means to be human, and what our actual place in the universe is.

Individual people also have differing views on the meaning of life itself. Some of us often wonder why we live and what the point is of our existence. Others just enjoy or suffer what life throws at them. Some believe that physical life is all there is and that life is just a random accident. Others believe that we were all created by a God or gods and are more than the animals, indeed that we are in dominion over them; also that human life is part of a divine plan and in living it we are being tested by this higher creator being.

What I can say, though, is that whatever the different outward form and words of the belief, there are at the core more similarities than differences. All religions or belief systems, organized or just faith-based, do believe in creation and some continuation after physical death. The aspect that survives is generally considered to be the spirit or the soul of the individual. After death this part of us is supposed to leave the body and move on to a higher plane or different dimension.

At this point it gets rather interesting. Beliefs about this moving on, where we go and for what purpose, are subject to many variations. Different realities could be indicated in the different theories of what happens after physical death. There are also several different inter-pretations of the various possibilities we do see reflected back. There are many scientific theories, covering interesting alternatives, which I shall look at later. There is often, but not always, a tension between belief and physics. All that can be said is that for most humans, unlike other animals, there seems to be a belief in something extra, alongside the physical body. There is often belief both in a spirit or soul, and in some sort of progression after physical death.

How did we get here?

How did we come to inhabit earth? There is a scientific belief that all of the universe, including ultimately ourselves, came into existence by chance. This is supposed to have happened billions of years ago. Conversely, the belief system some of us have adopted will give us religious, faith-based, answers to this question. For instance, I was taught that God made me and all around me. Could that actually be the whole answer? It is worth pointing out that science can define what human beings are biologically, but cannot yet properly explain what human life is all about.

Human construction

What we are, on one level, can be reduced to our basic human biology. We are told that our biological bodies are made of flesh and blood. This means a combination of organic biological systems and substances. We have a bony body skeleton which acts as a strong framework for the rest of the bodily systems. We have muscles which enable the skeletal framework to move around. Other complex bodily systems interact, to enable us to breathe, take nourishments from food, breed and so on. Our human brain, arguably a sort of human computer in our head, seemingly co-ordinates all of our body functions as well as allowing us to think. All of this body framework is covered with skin or flesh. We are seemingly a complete autonomous system.

On the next level down, these individual working components of our bodies themselves consist of a complex of biochemical and neurological systems. A heart pumps our blood round our body performing many functions, the most important being supplying oxygen to our brain. Lungs, and our breathing function, bring the much needed oxygen into our system. We have many internal organs that all have a different job to do. The organic systems in our bodies and minds seem to interact together to make us us. We are conceived, born, live and die to the tune of these biochemical and neurological systems.

How is it that our bodies are constructed as they are? The question of where our body design came from, whether it be wholly a product of random evolution, or has been designed by a higher being, I will look at later. But for now all we can say that it seems to be quite a well-functioning organic machine, usually fit for purpose.

But back again to basics. On the truly fundamental level, our bodies, indeed all living things, are constructed from different types of cells. There are different cells for different functions. Although every cell is the same genetically in an individual, every group of cells is slightly differently set up, or so-called 'differentiated', for those different body parts or functions. These cells are constructed internally, within the body, and constantly renewed. What we need for our cells to repair and multiply is taken into our body via the food we eat and the water we drink. These ingested substances are then broken down into the chemical compounds, vitamins, minerals and other nutrients that are needed for our health and well-being. These food-sourced, chemical compounds are therefore obtained from our natural world. We grow or harvest the food we need, to give us what our bodies require. We ingest our food and it is chemically broken down by our stomach juices into the compounds needed for growth, maintenance and survival. We are what we eat.

To delve deeper, these chemical compounds from which the cells are fashioned can themselves be broken down. They are constructed from many different molecules. Every molecule consists of combinations of the atoms of more basic substances, called elements. These elements make up our physical world. They are naturally occurring substances: things like iron, hydrogen and sodium and carbon. They have been on the earth from its birth. The elements have then combined together over time to make the more complex compounds from which our bodies, and in fact all around us, are constructed. This is school textbook stuff, but the bottom line is, that actually we are therefore nothing more physically than a bunch of combined, naturally occurring, elements. This is our first certain reality. We are made of what the earth is made of.

Our atomic structure

Fundamentally, all earth's elements, thus we ourselves, are made from atoms. Atoms are the basic building blocks of everything in the universe. Every element has a different atomic structure; there are well over 100 of them. They were fused into being from the most simple atoms in the nuclear reactor of the sun, before the earth was formed. These range from hydrogen, which has the most simple basic atomic structure, to the heavy, so-called radioactive, metals like plutonium, which are very complex structures. They are called radioactive because they are so complex and unstable that they can easily be made to decay, releasing their energy relatively easily but with potentially destructive consequences to things around them. In fact the whole world, living and non-living, is actually made of atoms of elements -in different combinations. For instance, each molecule of water, which accounts for much of our bulk, is made of a combination of two hydrogen atoms and one oxygen atom.

For many years atoms were considered the smallest possible unit, or building block, of matter known to man. Splitting the atom was a major quest for many years. It was considered to be impossible. Finally when scientists were able to split it, they found even smaller building blocks of matter. Atoms were found to consist of different combinations of smaller particles called protons, neutrons and electrons (plus some very weird particles which need not concern us here yet). For instance, hydrogen has one proton (positive charge) in its nucleus and one electron (negative charge) circling. Plutonium has ninety-four of each.

This may sound reassuringly complex and solid, but then you have to consider what these smaller particles are actually themselves made of. This is where it gets really interesting. At this, the high end of physics, as you stray into the realms of the really serious stuff, the scientific certainties that we have all grown up with begin to look less certain.

When I was growing up, the old school textbook pictures of atoms had, in the middle of the diagram, a collection of small round things lumped together. This was the atomic nucleus and consisted of protons and neutrons. Protons were shown having a positive charge and neutrons being shown as having no charge at all. Circling the nucleus, rather like the earth circles the sun, was one or many electrons represented by little balls. These had a negative charge. The combination of the proportions of protons in the nucleus and the number of electrons circling defined what sort of element atom it was. For example, hydrogen atoms have only one electron and one proton, oxygen atoms have eight of each. The components of the atom whiz around in lots of empty space. The atoms, even in this old model, were mostly space and relatively minute components. This seemed very simple, but it got more complicated.

Whole teams of scientists from all over the world worked on the great goal of splitting of the components of the atom. They hoped that this would be a step in understanding what the big picture of life was about, scientifically. Some, of course, just wanted to use the knowledge to make weapons of mass destruction. Eventually they found that electrons, protons and neutrons were themselves all made up of other, smaller, vibrating particles of energy called quarks. Since then other sub-atomic energy particles have been detected. Now there appear to be several different types and sizes of quarks, leptons and other strange particles. Things became more complicated not easier. At this point no one had actually seen one of these minute particles. Their presence had just been detected by experimental means (seeing remnants and debris). Certainties that we had been brought up with began to waver. These quarks are just different sorts of pulses of energy. Also, in practice, things are more complex than little ball-shaped things circling around another ball-shaped thing, but we will deal with that later.

Thus the electron of our atoms is made of a combination of pulses of energy, as are the protons and neutrons in the nucleus. We are made at base of nothing more than these atoms in different combinations. So the bottom line is that we are made of nothing more than just combinations of energy pulses. All we are is energy pulses in combination. That cannot be stressed enough. We, and the world around us, are ultimately made of vibrating pulses of energy and lots of empty space. Whatever our actual origins, the reality is that we, and all contained in the universe are actually just made of vibrating energy. Not only are we energy, we are part of a gigantic energy field. We humans are electrical beings within this field. This is mainstream scientific fact and is the result of decades of experiment and observation by the cream of scientific minds.

How this affects our understanding of reality is studied by those in a branch of high level physics and maths. It is called quantum mechanics. Quantum mechanics is the study of those itsy bitsy things that we, and the whole known universe, are made of. These are the quanta-parcels of vibrating energy. In looking at the fine detail of what physicists now know, we find that text book certainties that we were taught in schools suddenly become a bit wobbly. For instance, as I consider in more depth later in this book, the electron is sometimes observed doing really strange things, which seemingly contradict the basic laws of physics as we understood them to be. For example: by simply observing it, its path or velocity can be changed. Even more strangely, it can sometimes seem to be in two places at once. Does this mean that theoretically we could also be in two places at once?

What we mere mortals have been taught is simply not the whole story. If the electron, the vital part of our atomic structure, does not always follow the known laws of physics, what else may not?

Even more interestingly, science does not know for sure why the energy of our atoms becomes seemingly solid matter, or has mass. There has been an on-going search for the so-called 'god' particle or field, that would allow this to happen. At the time of writing, scientific researchers think they have found something they are calling the Higgs Boson, or Higgs field, which may answer this.

Can we be sure we are real?

It is worth mentioning also that, in understanding that we are only actually made of pinches of energy, other interesting questions about our reality come to light. How can we know that we are not just holograms or even a gigantic video game? How do we know that we are 'real'? Interestingly, this may not have occurred to most of us before the advent of holograms and computer generated simulations. Some of the ancient philosophers did however consider that it was a possibility; they understood that the material world may not be real. They, of course, did not know about holograms or computers. How can we then, if we are only made of energy, be really sure we actually exist? Whatever society and the text books say, we cannot actually be sure. Philosophers have been debating this for hundreds, if not thousands of years. On a day-to-day basis it does not even cross our minds.

Surprisingly, the answer is that actually we cannot really know, we can only believe that we are 'real' because we feel real. We feel pleasure, pain, love and hate. We hurt if we fall over. We feel we are alive, our senses lead us to believe that we are. We see other people around us and interact with them all the time. How can we not be who we think we are? I certainly never doubted the standard perception of reality whilst I was growing up. Even asking such a question as this would have branded me as bonkers.

As I came to understand next, all these feelings, emotions, awareness, pleasure and pain are seemingly only generated in the brain. Without the brain they would simply not occur. Our sense organs and nervous system feed the information about how our body is interacting with the world all around us into our brains. Our minds then make sense of the information. For instance, if we damage our body, our nerve endings send this information to our brain. Our brains register this as pain, then we think we feel it at the damage point. Although it feels real, the feeling of pain is generated in our minds not actually at the damage point.

The best consensus is that we can only know that we are 'real' because we do have minds. We do feel emotional pain and pleasure and we learn and make decisions – that is, we are aware. We know that we are conscious beings, whatever the true status of the world around us. We are conscious that we exist. That consciousness is what defines us. As the great Philosopher René Descartes said – "I think, therefore I am". He also emphasized that in fact our sense organs can mislead us; our minds are the only thing we can count on.

The truth is, we are just vibrating, interacting pulses of energy, who are part of a bigger universal energy field. We are also intelligent animals, living in the biosphere of earth. These are our seemingly certain realities. We were taught only that we lived on God's earth and were made in his image. These two positions need not necessarily contradict each other, as I discovered later.

When we look around us and think about who and what we are, this possible aspect of reality is puzzling. Around us are other people, loved ones, buildings, trees, fields, animals and other things, seemingly solid. It is hard to think of it all as only vibrating energy; indeed it is an almost impossible concept for a human mind to get around. It all looks and feels very substantial. We ourselves have almost never doubted that we are solid beings, who know we exist in a solid world because we interact with it. How could this possibly work? How could it all be no more than vibrating energy?

Why do we feel solid? Apparent solidity, I am told, is a matter of comparative densities. Things of a denser atomic structure (a bigger nucleus and more electrons) are apparently more solid than those comparatively less dense. My desk feels solid because the atomic structure of the compounds that make up the wood are stronger/denser than those of the piece of paper on my desk. This is, theoretically, why my paper does not fall though the desk. What about us?

Why don't we merge into things of a similar density to ourselves? I am told that our molecules are attracted to each other and exclude normal particles of other material from the space around them. High energy particles can get through. For instance, a bullet can pass through a body.

Aspects of reality

- We are physical entities living in the biosphere of a planet called Earth. We refer to ourselves as Human Beings. Humanity defines itself, and separates itself into individuals, because of different physical appearances, and differences in personality and thinking.

- It is our mental characteristics, our human minds, that make us who we are. They make us different from everyone else, even if we look similar. Identical twins may look exactly the same, but they are different and separate people.

- We have either been created by a God or outside agency, or we are a random accident of physical forces and blind evolution. Until we know which, we cannot be sure of what happens after physical death, if anything.

- Despite what we see when we look around us, we, and the earth are made only of pure vibrating energy. We only know we are 'real' because we think. Whether that is the whole sum of reality or not, remains to be seen.

Were we taught this at school? Absolutely not. This understanding though, and the questions it poses, are a vital first step in our quest for the truth. The next logical question that I asked myself was, where does this thinking mind actually come from?

CHAPTER TWO

Thoughts on thoughts

One of the most important insights that we can take from the last chapter is that the essence of our humanity – what makes us us – lies somewhere in the nature of our physical brain and the thinking mind it seems to generate. Our individual brains also make us the separate, individual, people we are. They differentiate us from all the other people around us.

When I was growing up we just assumed that the mind was part of the physical body, part of the allegedly God-created package we call a human being. Thinking and learning were just something that you did. Thoughts were also to be censored for temptation and sin. They were never assumed to be the one thing that defined you as real. The truth is that we make sense the whole of reality only through our minds. It cannot be emphasized enough that it is only by our thoughts and awareness, seemingly generated from this mind, that we know, for sure, that we exist.

So the next important questions I asked myself concerned the structure and function of this brain; the most important of these being, is the human mind something generated only, and wholly, from the physical human brain? Or could it be something quite separate? To tackle this question, I looked next at how the brain works, and where our thoughts, that make us us, are theoretically supposed to come from.

What does the physical brain do?

To get some sort of clarity, we have to look at what the human brain does and how it actually works. There seem to be two main types of brain function.

Firstly, the so-called deep brain co-ordinates the physical functions of the human body. It organizes our movements, walking, sleeping, the beating of our heart, our breathing, all our neurological and endocrinal systems. It does this without us being aware of it at all. It is like an organic computer.

Secondly, the brain also has a thinking and communicating mind function. It does seem to be the source of our thoughts and memories, and beyond that our consciousness or awareness. As stated before, our individual thinking brains/minds define who we are as individuals.

Starting from birth, if you remember, the new born baby does not concern itself about whether it exists or not, because it is not yet aware of itself as a separate entity. It does not have the knowledge. It operates on automatic reflexes and instincts. It does not yet, as we define it, think. Awareness and understanding gradually develop as it grows and takes in information from its surroundings. At a certain point it will realize that it exists as a separate entity within a world. It moves beyond mere instinct and becomes aware. How is that step taken? When does existing and taking in information change to becoming an aware, thinking and conscious being? The really big question is then: when and how does a physical brain, the lump of grey matter at the very top of our bodies, become a thinking, self-aware mind? As a corollary to that, the difficult question, which I look at later in this chapter, is: can this 'mind' be actually separated from our biological brain?

The structure of the human brain

To even start to understand this, we have to understand a little of how the human brain works. We have probably all seen anatomy textbook pictures of the inside of the human brain. They call it grey matter and it looks like squished up sausages crammed into the human skull. There are various named parts such as the cerebral hemispheres, the lobes, left brain and right brain and the cerebellum. Different parts of the brain have particular functions. For instance, the hypothalamus collects the information arriving into the brain from the sensory organs. With any action or interaction various parts of the brain activate and work together. It is worth mentioning that, even now, the brain's total functions, and the way that the various parts work together, are not yet totally understood. There is at the moment much research going on into the matter.

In practical terms, the human brain is a very complex mechanism that co-ordinates our physical movements and interprets input from our senses. It is hard-wired, like any machine, with connections between the sensory inputs (senses) and motor outputs (what our bodies do). It is also in some sense free flowing, as through life it has the capacity to make new connections. It is also fixed as to the physical grey matter that is actually there. It is the brain that does the organizing for our body. It initiates our actions and controls movements. It takes in information from the physical world through sight, sound, smell and touch. It can be seen as an efficient biological, computer-like machine.

How is the brain supposed to work?

Biologically, and this is a gross simplification, but bear with me, the textbook mechanics seem to be as follows: the brain is a buzzing network of specialized nerves called neurons and synapses (connections). Neurons work to transmit information within, and between, areas of the brain. These are continually functioning even when we sleep. Appropriate areas of the brain are stimulated and linked to perform every function required by our bodies. There are two main types of neuron. Sensory neurons carry signals to the brain from the other parts of the body. These tell the brain what is in the world around it. What we touch, smell and feel are reported back to the brain. Motor neurons carry the signals from the brain to the muscles, skin, glands and so on. This causes them to react and move, if appropriate, to do what we want or need them to do. Thus we walk and talk and physically react to the information gleaned from the sense organs.

As mentioned before, we get information into the brain through our sense organs. These include eyes, ears, nose and skin. Our brain enales us to make sense of the world through these inputs. What we see and hear and feel are efficiently processed. The results give us our world view and the information to enable our physical body to move safely within its physical environment. Our brain can only process what it registers. Because we are taking in so much information constantly, we are not consciously aware of all of it. If the quality of the sense organs is flawed we may not get the whole picture. This is why sometimes people seem not to see or hear or smell the same things. Deaf people are not aware of sound, blind people cannot know colour and so on. But even a small variation in quality of sense organs can make a difference to what we actually perceive in the world.

Anyway, it is through these sense mechanisms that we are aware of, and feel part of, the world. For example, the brain uses pain to alert us to problems. Interestingly, and tellingly, as mentioned before, we feel pain actually only in our minds rather than at the site of the hurt and distress. Nerve impulses travel up to the brain, are decoded, and sent down to the pain site, instructing us to 'feel' pain. We also feel pleasure in the brain. All sensations and emotions actually only become reality in the brain.

There is a supposedly 'thinking' part of the brain which includes the frontal lobes. These deal with the higher level functions of the brain. These include the processing of experiences and turning them into memories. The memory function of the brain seems to be one of the greatest mysteries. It was once thought that only the temporal lobes seem to store those memories, rather like a computer database. In some scientific circles this is now being questioned. Where memory is actually located is not clearcut. There is even a theory that memory may be stored in every cell of the body. There is some proof of this in the strange phenomena occurring when people receive heart transplants. When major organs are transplanted, recipients have sometimes reported acquiring new character traits, skills and tastes, as if from the donor. Anyway, if you lose the thinking brain, the body may still work, but it would be a mere machine. So-called brain dead, your physical body would still work but you would not be you at all.

How thoughts are generated

How are our individual thoughts generated within this brain? The answer is that the whole process of the brain is managed bio-chemically. There are chemicals which generate an electrical signal. That is, the body's own chemistry is utilized to make electrical charges, through which information travels. The neurons transmit their information by using this bio-electrochemical process.

How does this work? I am told the process goes like this: neurons and nerve cells have a balance of ions inside and outside. Ions are electrically charged particles. The relative numbers of these charged particles control the potential, that is how much electrical energy, the cell has. To pass a signal down the cell, some sort of stimulus, for example, touch, causes a chain of events whereby neurotransmitters tell the cell to open up certain channels to let the sodium ions in. The ions have an electrical charge so that the voltage of the cell increases. Once it reaches a certain threshold point, all/most of the channels open at once and there is a massive increase in energy which can be passed down the cell very quickly. When it reaches the end of this process, it releases more neurotransmitters to another nerve and the process starts again. Our thoughts are electrically powered.

This means that our thoughts are just another form of energy. Emotions are energy, memories are stored as energy. They are all nothing but electronic pulses. Brain waves can be measured. You must have all heard of Alpha and Theta waves. We have all seen hospital dramas on the TV when we know that the patient has died when the brainwaves stop going up and down and start flat-lining. No brainwave means no active brain. No active brain means no conscious person can be said to exist. On a more positive note, in some experimental circles, electrodes are now being implanted into the brain to try and interpret some brainwaves into particular words, to help those who have lost the ability to speak. Whether this will be successful or not remains to be seen.

The subconscious brain

As well as organizing the functions of our body and being host to our conscious thoughts, our brain also has a mechanism called the subconscious. It is like a large database that we are not aware of on a day-to-day basis, but which is essential to our functioning in the world. In it is stored all of our previous life experiences, all our skills, all that we have learnt, all of the situations we have ever faced and all of the images that we have ever seen. It may also carry our belief system. It is a mechanism which influences and guides our conscious thought processes. We are not usually aware of it on a day-to-day basis. It stores and processes all the data our sense organs are taking in continually. We would be overwhelmed if we consciously received all the information at once. Our conscious brain accesses what it needs for day-to-day interaction in the world.

Where do our personalities come from?

How do we, as individuals, get our own particular physical brains? We are, of course, born with them. Every baby inherits generally, at random, as with all other parts of the body, fifty percent of genes from each parent. The quality of a person's brain will, as everything in our body does, vary from person to person. The different quality and quantity of our neurons and sense organs gives us our different abilities and computing brain power. If one parent has particular talents because they have a brain that is rich with the neurons that, for instance, give very good colour sight, you may inherit those genes and also have the same talents. Some physical abilities and talents are also determined by the quality and quantity of certain parts of the brain. If you have a brain that is genetically set up to be efficient with physical motor skills, then you are more likely to take an interest in, and be good at participating in physical sports.

But because at the moment of conception you receive fifty percent of active genes from both parents, the ones that go into your physical make up may not contain those particular genes. You may be genetically lucky or unlucky. The alternative characteristics, which you may have inherited, will lay dormant in your cells as recessive genes. Your children may, of course, inherit them from you. I can see traits of both my parents in myself and certainly in my children. Some things, I am told, come straight from my grandmothers on both sides!

So we know we are all born with physical characteristics, which may influence what we can do, and our awareness or consciousness, which may or may not be generated wholly from our physical brain. These factors combined together form our personality. Our personality is how we are judged to be individuals. The other factor that also influences our personality is acquired knowledge. This we get though personal experience, and information about the world, programmed into us by our parents and the education system. We are, as individuals, only the total sum of these processes.

Nature or nurture?

There is actually another, ongoing, debate about what makes an individual who they are. This is the 'nature versus nurture' argument. Whether it is nature (our genetic inheritance) or nurture (our environment and the way we have been brought up) which is the prime cause of our personality has been argued about for years. Most people now understand it is a combination of both, even though they may argue over the degree that we are most influenced by either. Anyway, in the end, all these factors combine to make us us.

Fixed or flexible?

Is this brain, which generates the mind, fixed? It was generally assumed that the physical brain you were born with, you were stuck with. There is a relatively new scientific discipline called neuro-plasticity. This studies the brain's capacity to change. It is proposed that not only can the brain influence thought, but that thoughts themselves can actually change the structure of our brain. It has been found that, contrary to previous assumptions, the adult brain remains relatively plastic. It can, in some circumstances, repair damaged regions, re-zone regions, expand other regions, and change the linking circuitry that enables us to feel and think. If this is possible, then could the thoughts that instigate changes come wholly from within the brain that is being changed? It is perhaps some evidence that the mind/brain is two co-operating systems rather than one. It is worth noting that Buddhism has taught for at least two thousand five hundred years, that the mind is an independent force that can be harnessed to bring about physical change.

The great brain debate

When looking at the human brain, a very interesting question arises. That is, are the co-ordinating physical brain (and indeed physical body), and the thinking mind, part of the same thing, one system? Or are they two different, but linked, systems working together? This is a difficult question that has been argued over, by brilliant minds, for thousands of years. Unsurprisingly there is not one absolute consensus among scientists or philosophers, with each other or between either camp.

This contentious issue does then naturally lead the way to the key question of whether our physical biology is the whole story of who we are. If it is, then we are just as we perceive ourselves to be; that is, just intelligent, evolved animals living on and as part of a randomly evolved ecosystem, on an accidentally-occurring planet. However, if thoughts and self-awareness can be shown not just to be a function of the biological brain, but something else entirely, this then becomes a different matter. Could our awareness, or conscious-ness, which makes us us, originate or come in from elsewhere? If so, then that could indicate a different, more complex, bigger picture of existence. It lays open the possibility of the existence of a soul. It also lays open a possibility of other unseen dimensions that the soul can go back to after death. It comes back again to the basic question, what precisely is thought? Even more importantly, what actually is awareness?

Could we be just our genes?

For instance, some scientists and philosophers think that we are only biological beings, determined by our genetics and the interaction with our environment, which we shape according to our genetically programmed brains. This is called the Determinist view. The interesting corollary to that is, if the decisions that we make are all biologically driven, can we be responsible for them? We could say that our genetics made us do it, when accused of murder, or indeed any crime. This is patently absurd, but logical if we follow the pure Determinist line of thought. It would require a rethink on crime and punishment if it were wholly true. No one could be blamed for anything they did.

Could this actually be the whole story? This is where the concept of human, so-called, 'free will' is often brought to our attention. 'Free will' is the ability of humans to override any Determinist forces and make choices. It can be seen in two ways. It is either a genetic function of the developed mind, or it is a gift from God.

Also, others feel that there is something extra, above and beyond the genetically programmed brain, which makes us what we are as individuals, besides nature or nurture. It is felt that the high level of consciousness exhibited by mankind is simply too complex to be a product of a random biological evolutionary process. If this is true then this may give us clues to a whole new understanding of a greater reality than that which we can see at present.

There are, of course, many different theories between either end of this argument. The truth has implications for the creation of truly thinking computers, or artificial intelligence, as well as for an understanding of the true nature of man. It is worth mentioning that, as yet, no computer has properly exhibited truly independent thinking, above and beyond its programming. Perhaps it will never be possible without an extra something which we humans seem to have.

The official scientific explanations for the workings of the brain are still incomplete. We simply do not know the whole story. All we can now do is look further for other clues around us to what is really happening, in our quest to understand what, and who, we humans really are.

Aspects of reality

- All of the matter of the universe, at atomic level, consists of nothing but vibrating pulses of energy. Out of these vibrating pulses of energy is formed a physical body, including a biological brain. This brain determines, as individuals, who we are.

- The physical structure of our brains comes from our genetics.

- From this brain somehow thoughts, awareness, consciousness and personality are seemingly bio-chemically generated.

- There is a serious debate about whether the mind and brain are one system or two separate systems in co-operation.

- Some people believe that the thinking and aware mind (consciousness) cannot just be a function of the biological brain, but must come from elsewhere. We are not just biological beings.

- If that is the case, if consciousness can be separable from the physical brain, and could have come in from elsewhere, then from where could it have come and what could its purpose be? Could it even be a soul as described by religious thinkers?

The key reality conundrum here may lie in the real understanding of this so-called consciousness or awareness. If it is not wholly generated within the brain, but comes in from elsewhere, what could be its true nature? Also as a corollary, there is problem with the understanding of the very nature of human free will. An understanding of consciousness, our thinking self-awareness, may just give us the clues we need to move forward on our quest. Certainly a fascination with the concept of the nature of our consciousness and what its existence meant, was the trigger that set me finally on my path towards finding some possible answers to questions about the big picture of reality.

CHAPTER THREE

A question of consciousness

As children and adults living in the day-to-day world we take this so-called consciousness, if it concerns us at all, for granted. Certainly, that it was special, or unusual, never crossed my mind. After all, thinking, being aware of all around us, is something that we do all the time. An often unasked question is, how do we know that others around us are conscious? The surprising answer is that we only know that to be a fact because they communicate with us by written, or spoken, word. Speech is a way of converting thoughts into sound vibrations, which is then interpreted back into speech by our brains. Only by knowing others are thinking can we understand them to be conscious. We can also access other people's consciousness through their written words.

But it is still a great mystery how, or why, our biological brain, a mass of grey matter, a collection of neurons, powered by electro-chemical impulses, becomes a thinking being. Not only that, but a being that is aware of itself, and its place in the world. It is amazing when you think about it.

It can be easy to understand the mechanical role of the brain in using the external senses (eyes, ears, nose, mouth and skin) to make sense of the world that it finds around it. If you remember, the brain is, at a fundamental level, an organizing machine, enabling the human body to move and interact within its environment. It is also relatively simple to see this brain storing the images and impressions it receives in a sort of database. It can also then be seen to be storing memories and making decisions based on the information it receives via the cerebral cortex. The tricky bit is, when does this passive data and image storing machine take the next step into becoming an aware and thinking entity? What makes us different from mere advanced computers who do all that processing but are not capable of independent thought? Do all living brains, even those of primitive animals, 'think', or do they just react to their instincts and the circumstances around them? Are we unique in being aware of ourselves as individuals? Or are we special in being both aware and thinking beings, conscious that we are alive and living in an interactive society? These are all questions I look at in this chapter.

What is consciousness?

This special sort of awareness we are talking about is known as consciousness. The working definition of consciousness is the most difficult concept to pin down of all. What do we actually mean by it? Of course, on one level being conscious can just mean being awake, aware of our surroundings, aware of colours, and so on. How can it be defined exactly? That is the tricky question. There are many text book definitions. The next level of consciousness also involves being aware of one's identity as a thinking being. This is the level we are most concerned with, as it involves observing, and having thoughts that are not just necessary for bodily function, maintenance and survival. Also, the capacity for independent, abstract thought is vital in this definition; we are not just machines reacting to the world around us. Perhaps the most important function of this sort of consciousness is actually the capacity to ask, why? That is, we are conscious of ourselves as separate, thinking, questioning, interacting human beings. Just knowing that we are thinking human beings, is being conscious in a way that separates us from the other animals around us.

Those studying the matter have criteria by which they define such consciousness. Generally these criteria involve a mix of factors. These include using language to communicate and being aware of the passing of time. Fully conscious beings also remember things, rather than instinctively know, for example, when seasons are due to change.

They look forward to abstract future events like birthdays. They make sense of the world using past memories. They recognize their images in the mirror. They know themselves to be individuals. Some believe that our very essence of who we are as individuals is inseparable from this consciousness.

Is anyone else conscious?

Are any other beings around us conscious in that special way? Animals are aware of their surroundings, but they are not necessarily conscious. They are not thinking about the meaning of life, or what they have to do next week. They are not concerning themselves with tomorrow or yesterday, only what is needed for survival today. They are not worrying about appearances, or the state of the world. Their animal instincts and biologically driven hormones guide their behaviour.

It is worth mentioning however that recent studies have found that many animals have more, lower level, consciousness than was previously thought. Even cows form friendship groups and bear grudges. Elephants have prodigious memories. Killer whales co-operate in complex ways to catch seals. But generally even the more complex animals (apes, dogs, cats and horses) are not considered wholly conscious beings as we are. The famous naturalist Charles Darwin studied animal emotions in the 19th century. He found that higher animals, at least, felt emotions: sorrow, rage and so on. Any cat owner these days might report that cats exhibit feelings such as frustration and happiness, as well as the above. This is not the same as the capacity for abstract thought, though. The sort of thinking consciousness, or self-awareness, that we have is special. As far as we know we are the only species in the world to have this gift fully. Although some higher primates can be shown to have a degree of it, human beings are the only ones considered to have it completely.

As mere products of our biology and environment, you would think that our behaviour would be guided mainly by those two factors. In practice though, we seem to be able consciously to over-ride our natural, biologically-driven instincts. Some people also feel that this is the same as 'free will'. We can make decisions, which may or may not be logical. Unlike most other animals, we choose to do things other than those which are necessary for survival. We create things of beauty for their own sakes and we make war on others for reasons other than for sheer necessity. Most importantly of all, we do have the capacity to question the world around us, not to just react to it.

Why does consciousness matter?

Consciousness matters because it is what makes us different from machines or holograms and computer generated imaginary people. If consciousness, or the essence of us that seems not just biologically based, can be proved to be separate from our biological, body operating brain, then this is an important step forward. Could this essence/consciousness be the same thing as a religious, or even non-religious, soul? This question has huge implications for our understanding of the actual nature of reality.

One system or two?

The key question again then, is; is it possible to separate the computer-like functions of the brain, that operate the body and take in information, from that extra bit of us that does the thinking and being aware of ourselves as individuals? Can consciousness be seen to be an add-on to the biological brain, or is it part of the same physical system? What proof could there be either way? As mentioned before, this mind/body debate is aeons old. Is it one system or two? Can the mind exist without the body? We do know that the mind seemingly cannot exist without the body organizing part of the brain (brain dead). But the body, in some circumstances, can seem to exist in a long term vegetative state without the thinking part of the brain. Is that some sort of proof of two separate systems?

Artificial intelligence

To make some sense of this, it is useful to compare human intelligence with machine intelligence. The study of so-called 'Artificial intelligence' illustrates the difference between conscious and non-conscious entities. What is the difference between a human brain and a computer brain? Both take in data, both are powered by a form of electricity. The difference is both consciousness, and our ability to override our data. We can harm ourselves. We can take decisions that harm our best interests, we can fall in love. We will react to different events, not just according to logic, but according to the state of our minds. Machines can only act on the data input according to their programmed instructions. Will machines ever be able to think and be self-aware? All they are doing at the moment is mechanically processing vast quantities of information and synthesizing this to produce output or answers. This may look like thinking but it is not. Then again the great and the good are divided between those who think machines achieving proper consciousness is only a question of time, and those who think consciousness is different, and it can never happen.

There is a useful analogy called 'The Chinese Room'. This involves a sealed room with a hatch into an outer chamber. In the sealed room there are symbols and a book of instructions. Someone passes other symbols though the hatch and a person in the sealed room matches the symbols according to the book of instructions and passes out those matched. The point is that the matcher does not have to understand what the symbols mean to produce an output. This equates to how a computer processes information, but does the brain work just like that? Is our book of instructions part of our brain, or does it come from elsewhere? Will more powerful computers of the future become self-aware? Is it just a question of inputting a critical mass of data?

To recap, it is not known what actually makes our human, data absorbing, brain take the leap into the value-added thinking that being a conscious being involves. It is not yet fully understood if consciousness is just an advanced part of the human animal brain, or something separate. The real puzzle then is, is our conscious mind just a biological function of our human brain? This is still a great scientific puzzle that occupies a lot of the hyper-intelligent today. It also occupied the ancient philosophers and probably a lot of the modern ones as well. What proof do we have either way?

The view of science

Many scientists tend to believe that these higher level thoughts and awareness are just a normal biological function of the well-developed human brain. This would have given us, as primitive man, an evolutionary advantage in predicting future events and hazards and organizing ourselves . Natural selection would have ensured that those more capable of surviving would have been more likely to survive and breed. If higher levels of thought had been an advantage, those capable of doing it would have had a genetic advantage which will have been passed on. Those not capable of thinking and planning would have been more likely to have been destroyed in hard times.

The view of faith

Religion tells us something different. I was taught at school that God created us in his own likeness. A soul is given to each person at the moment of conception. This is added on to the mere biological human being and makes us human. Our genes and inherited characteristics could make us tend to behave in certain ways (almost a Determinist View), not always good. Our souls could give us the capacity to override those genetics if we choose. These souls were separate from our body and went back to God after death. We were given 'free will' to enable us to over ride our genetic-based behaviour if needed. This scenario does, however, assume a separation between mind and body, at least that part of the mind that is extra to the base, organizing biological machine function.

An alternative view

Many 'alternative' thinkers today also believe that we do have an extra dimension that works with our biological brain to make us us. It is sometimes also called a soul, but not necessarily a religious one. It comes from a higher dimension, from outside our biological selves.

Any discussion on consciousness will always raise more questions than it is capable of answering. Also, as the Dalai Lama said in his book *The Art of Happiness*, "...in modern Western society, there seems to be a powerful cultural conditioning that is based on science. But in some instances, the basic premises and parameters set up by western science can limit your ability to deal with certain realities..."

Looking beyond both conventional and unconventional teaching, is it possible to scientifically prove that consciousness is added on to our biological brain as an extra? Can it be shown to come from elsewhere, rather than being just a biological function of our genetically determined brain? The short answer is probably no, or rather not yet. Possible non-religious 'elsewheres' are being revealed with new theories on the scientific origins and structure of the universe though. These I look at later. All I can say now is that it is in these unknowns that we are given a sight of the reflections of possible different realities from those which we have previously been told exist.

Proof that consciousness continues after death

Suspending, for the moment, all thought of religious faith, and scientific proof, there is a wealth of anecdotal evidence for the continuation of consciousness when the physical body ceases. Whatever the mainstream of science and faith say, many ordinary people, from many different backgrounds, have experienced, and reported, phenomena over many years. These events form a compelling body of evidence for the separation of the conscious mind and the physical body.

There are two different such phenomena that are gaining more and more credence, usually despite the mainstream scientific cynicism. These are the so-called Near Death Experience (NDE) and Out of Body Experience (OBE). Both phenomena show that part of us, an aware part, can be shown to be capable of leaving the body. Both confirm that our consciousness may be separable from our physical body, in some continuing form.

Out of Body Experiences

These are said to happen when a person feels that some part of them has left their physical body, and is out and about in the world. They are usually floating about, and often observe their inert physical body where they last left it. They see their physical bodies lying down in the room below. They often see details in the room that they would not see from their prone position. This sometimes seems to happen accidentally in times of stress. Some people even claim to be able to do it at will. They leave their bodies and travel where they choose. This is called astral travel.

In fact there are many examples of ordinary, sensible, people experiencing out of body phenomena. Often they have been sceptical about such things, before it happens to them. My discussions with many people over the years have revealed more and more examples. It is much more common than you might imagine. Also, any trawl though the internet will reveal pages and pages of such reported incidents. None of this seems scientifically provable however. All people can attest to are things such as seeing friends doing things at a certain time, which is later verified, which they could not have possibly known unless they had been there to actually see what was going on.

For instance, even from among my friends and acquaintances there are some examples. Once, a former high level civil servant friend of mine, told me that in the process of the birth of her second child, she felt herself floating up to the left hand corner of her bedroom ceiling. She then proceeded to watch what went on below. She then returned to her body and completed the birth. This happened before she had had any drugs or pain killers which may have caused her to hallucinate. Another friend remembers leaving her body at a time of high stress and flying through the bedroom window. She flew around the local woods, returning to her inert body in her bed later. Other friends have given me similar examples. Many have been really sheepish when they have told me, as they felt admitting it made them look strange. These may seem trivial examples, but the point is they happened to a small sample of people I personally know, in the general population. There are many, many more people out there, who tell similar stories. There are just too many good examples for the experience to be only a result of overactive imaginations.

As a child I remember thinking I had got up in the morning and being aware that I was walking downstairs. On realizing that I was still asleep, I would return to my sleeping body in bed. Was that an out of the body experience? Just sleepwalking? A reflection of a different reality? Or was it just a childish dream? I now often wonder!

Near Death Experiences

These are said to occur when people are on the point of death, either due to an accident or severe illness. They are aware of leaving their bodies and moving away from them. In some cases, in hospital, this phenomenon seem to happen between the point of technical clinical death, and being revived. These cases are interesting because the death has often been confirmed from evidence on the hospital monitoring machines. It therefore cannot be dismissed as not actually having happened, as tended to happen previously.

Accounts vary as to details of what happens from then on, but there are common themes. People sometimes feel that they begin to travel upwards, encountering feelings of great peace. Some people see tunnels and lights, some mention meeting loved ones who had passed over already. Some even mention a life review. Having assumed they were dying, they then suddenly find themselves back into their bodies. Interestingly enough, some people say they were given a choice as to whether to return or not. When they resume consciousness, they sometimes report what they felt had happened to them. Often they can even tell the doctors and nurses working on them what had been said and done, whilst they were clinically dead.

Having, up until now, no current scientific validity, these happenings are often dismissed as being the product of over-active imaginations. There are those that say this phenomena is only a trick of the brain. They feel, indeed, that the mechanism to allow it may be hard-wired into our brains to make the acceptance of death easier. Is that likely? If it is, then what would be the evolutionary need for it?

These phenomena are, however, experienced by more people than care to openly admit, especially in public. Some parts of the medical profession are, however, also beginning to take them seriously. There are, even now, ongoing studies being conducted into this phenomenon by serious medical practitioners. In years past, an experience was often put down to hallucinations caused by the stress of the event or a side effect of the many painkillers involved. The thought was also that these people were not actually dead, or near death. Sophisticated monitoring machines now show that the people in question actually were dead.

Scientific investigation

Some doctors and scientists are actually trying to investigate the phenomena properly. For instance, cardiac arrest patients at the Southampton Hospital are being studied in death and resuscitation situations, to explore this very subject. The reports of the findings of the ongoing studies are being published by Doctor Sam Parnia.[1] These are particularly interesting, as the patients in question are closely monitored by machines, including an EEG (monitoring brainwaves). Studies have looked at those patients who are actually clinically dead, with the brain showing flat lines on the monitors. Many people report seeing things concealed on the top of cupboards in the room. These have been deliberately put there by the doctors for this purpose. The patient could not possibly have known they were there beforehand. When this Near Death Experience (NDE) has happened, the areas of the brain responsible for sustaining life, and the areas responsible for thought, have often been shown to have no measurable function at all.

Reported evidence

It has never happened to me, but another simple trawl though my close friends revealed several examples. Sometimes they revealed again that they had not ever told anyone before in case they were considered silly. For instance, a close friend's grandfather, who had had a heart attack, watched himself being worked on above his body

---

1   Near Death Experiences in *Cardiac Arrest and the Mystery of Consciousness*. Sam Parnia from the internet, also published in the medical journal *Resuscitation*.

and heard all conversations. Before it happened to him he was very much a sceptic. Another friend revealed that two of his close family members had had near death experiences many years ago. They had reported seeing the bright light, the tunnel upwards and meeting dead relatives.

There are many more credible experiences reported by credible people in the media and on the internet. These events happened to people who had no preconceived ideas that such things were possible. Before close electronic monitoring of the brain function, these experiences were usually always dismissed by doctors as dreams or hallucinations. Now technology actually shows that some people really have no brain function at all and are clinically dead when these near death phenomena occur. Although the human brain and mind still hold many mysteries, these events show that, in all probability, consciousness is not just a biological function of the brain. It does go on when our body ceases. If consciousness was only a function of the biological brain, the reported near death events could not be possible.

Although philosophers and alternative thinkers have always believed that it was a strong possibility, some of the scientific community involved in mind and consciousness studies are beginning to acknowledge that the thinking mind and the physical, organizing brain may be two systems, not one.

There is also an interesting, well-known but strange, mental condition, which also seems to give credence to the theory that the mind and personality are not just a simple function of the physical brain. This is called dissociative individual entity disorder. Also known as multiple personality disorder, it has been known about in the psychiatric profession for many years.

Sufferers have at least two, often more, distinct personalities or consciousnesses, inhabiting the same physical brain. They may have different voices, and even purport to be of different sexes. The consciousnesses have no awareness or recall of each other's actions or memories. This has often, but not always, been linked to trauma or abuse at a young age. What does it say about who we are, if several different personalities can exist in the same physical body?

Consciousness, or our thinking mind, can be seen to be separate from the higher brain functions. Also, as Near Death experiences show, it need not have the physical brain apparently working at all to exist.

This conclusion is a great stride forward in our journey. However the realization that consciousness, our very essence, can be seen to continue after death, poses more questions that have to be answered. If it is separate, why should this be so and where has it come from? What is the reason for it? What does it say about the true nature of us? What does it say for the true, big picture, nature of reality?

Aspects of reality

- We are not just biological beings; there seems to be part of us, our consciousness, that is separate from our physical bodies, whilst working in harmony with them.

- The idea of our essence, or consciousness, being separate from our biological bodies does give credence to the concept of a soul. Does this mean that the religious thinkers are correct?

- Where in reality could this soul have come from?

- The organized religions of the world have always maintained that we go on to some sort of afterlife after death. The possibility of the mechanism for an essence or soul, gives this more credence. Where could it be that we actually go?

- The alternative views of moving on to unknown dimensions also become possible.

- Some people believe that we re-incarnate. Some people believe our consciousness returns into a new body and we try again to improve ourselves until we reach perfection.

Which set of the many alternative scenarios are the most likely?

What clues are there in our own lives that could help to explain any of it? When people reject conventional religious beliefs they may often also reject the concept of a soul. If you have been taught that the world and universe is a certain way from early childhood it is hard to imagine alternatives. This is especially true in a society like ours that does not generally have open discussions on such matters.

It seems to me that the soul, our essence, can be seen to exist, whether or not it is the soul as described by the mainstream, or religious, thought. The existence of a spirit or soul, after all, is a strong reflection from our glitter ball of seemingly conflicting realities. In rejecting conventional religion we are not necessarily turning away from the concept of the soul. We are merely looking, as clear-sightedly as possible, beyond the mundane.

In considering our clues and evidence in our search for the truth about reality, we must look at what our society's conventional religions have to say about the soul and its continuance. What clues to the truth are there? Could they have been right after all?

CHAPTER FOUR

Religious clues

The realization that there was, after all, a possible mechanism enabling us to go on after physical death was, for me, a great leap forward in understanding. I felt it was a major breakthrough in my quest. This reality, of course, has been preached by those of a religious bent in our society, since long before the establishment of the Christian church. Other religions, and alternative thinkers, also hold this fact to be self-evident. We were also taught that it was a matter of faith, not science, that part of you would automatically move on after biological death. This non-physical part of you would return to your God or maker. That we all have a sort of soul which might move on whether you believed in the possibility or not, was simply not considered. What this could mean for the actual nature of reality, beyond that of conventional religious teaching, was not discussed.

Even assuming a soul, what evidence is there that we do move on to a different level of existence after death ? There are, if we look and listen, good clues, reflections, in our own culture that this does happen in some way. Without doubt there is a continuation of some sort. Our life essence, or soul, call it whatever you like, can be shown to go on after our physical death in some form. What the actual mechanism is, or why it happens, are other great mysteries. But because we cannot yet understand the mechanism, this does not mean it does not happen or exist.

A majority of people I have talked to, from all walks of life and levels of education, seem to believe that life continues in some form. They may disagree on the detail but, practically or instinctively, agree with the principle. There are those, of course, who think that the whole subject is ridiculous, and simply absurd. We must understand that for some people, unless they can see obvious scientific proof of anything, it cannot be true. They are entitled to this view. But for those of us that understand things to be different, we have to ask the next questions.

Can we believe in the religious views?

We must first ask, how far can we believe, or challenge, the conventional beliefs that we were brought up with? If continuation after death is a fact, could conventional Christian religious views actually be more accurate than anything science has to offer? This, I felt, needed to be explored. What follows is my understanding on the state of affairs. It does not pretend to be comprehensive or a textbook explanation. This is a personal journey; observations were taken from my own understandings, experiences and discussions with other people. It is worth pointing out here also that not believing in the conventional God, as written about in Holy Scriptures, does not necessarily mean that you do not believe in a divine being at all.

The Christian message

Although I am someone who has always asked awkward questions, it took me a long time to question our society's accepted religious dogma. I was, after all, brought up to believe it unquestioningly. The Christian message was drummed into us by church, school and society. Also, when I was growing up, conventional thinking did assume that the mainstream religious beliefs, as taught in school and accepted by our society, were all there were. Certainly, when I was at school I never really doubted what we were taught.

This was:

- That God made us, and all around us, to his own design and image.

- That there was a Holy Trinity of deities, God the Father, God the Son (Jesus) and God the Holy Spirit. These were all parts of the one God.

- God created the earth and populated it with plants, animals and mankind.

- We all have something called a soul. This soul was said to arrive into the physical body, sometime before or around the time of birth. At the point of death it leaves our body and goes back to our maker to be judged.

It was emphasized that we were put on earth as some sort of test. If we failed then the consequences would be severe. We would either be rewarded by heaven or sent down to hell. Not following the maker's absolute rules was described as sin. These ranged from severe, like murder, to minor, for example being rude. The priests, nuns and other religious personnel were somehow gate-keepers of your soul and the concept of sin (yours) and punishment were always on their minds. Hell was painted as dreadful; eternal fires were mentioned often. Heaven was similarly painted as idyllic and to be aimed for. Other organized religions, even those thousands of years old, were questionable or wrong. Their adherents would not be saved.

Somehow the morals and ethos of our society were also wound up in this Christian message. The ruling class was, in theory at least, Christian. Historically, such principles as, "The rich man at his castle and the poor man at his gate" had to be maintained. The messages of this religion captured the hearts and minds of the masses and were gradually taken up by the powers that be. In England the political establishment used the established church to help keep the social structure intact. The Kings developed alleged divine rights (rather in the ways of the ancient Egyptian Pharaohs) and the peasantry were kept in their place. This was far from the original Christian message.

Even challenging the status quo in society was seen as unchristian. The rather austere women who had charge of us at school seemed to take a grim satisfaction in frightening us, although what sins a bunch of innocent school girls could get up to (it was the 50's) was slightly puzzling. Personally, and probably heretically, I was also uneasy at some of the apparent contradictions. If God was love why was he allegedly so vengeful? If he made us and we were flawed, wasn't it his fault? If we were all created equal then why was there so much snobbery and hierarchy involved in the church and society?

The underlying message of Christianity, however, loving your neighbour, helping others, treating others as you yourself would be treated, and so on, is a good and useful road map to live a life. The organized church, which some people still feel to be immutable, is still a man-made construct.

But if we do acknowledge that, in all probability, consciousness goes on, then soul is as a good as any name for the conscious part of us that is not just biologically created by our genes. In accepting this, then a whole new road map for our journey of exploration opens up. Many different possibilities are spread before us. How can we work out which is the most likely? Is there only one answer? Is the religious truth we have all been taught at school and church actually anything like the way things really are? Was that unease I felt, even as a small child, based on anything?

The Soul

We must first ask, how is this soul defined? Most dictionaries define the religious soul along the lines of "The spiritual or immaterial part of a human being, sometimes thought of as immortal". The word immortal, meaning living for ever, being the key word. This implies that the soul does not die with you but goes on after your physical life. It is the non-physical part of you. Religiously, it is somehow responsible, above and beyond the physical body, for your conduct in this world. It can be seen as the mechanism which allows you to override your genetically produced brain and upbringing.

Most religions thus see the soul as the mechanism through which your actions, in life, will be judged by a higher being, after death. Could this be possible? To recap, if you accept that the Near Death and Out of Body experiences, are valid, then consciousness/essence can be seen to leave the body and go on in some form. The part of consciousness that is an extra to the physical body and travels beyond the body at death, could be called the soul. It is, after all, the essence of you. Whether it is the same as the soul as described by mainstream religion, is another matter.

Accepting this to be true does give rise to another set of difficult questions. Where could this consciousness/soul come from? Does its existence mean that God, as described in the Bible, may actually exist? Could God, or a creative force, exist, but not in the way as described? Did any of the Bible stories actually happen? Are they actual or anecdotal evidence? If not where could this soul/consciousness come from and go to after death?

Life after death

Mainstream religions have after all generally been saying, almost since the beginnings of recorded time, that we do go on after death. Even our pre-Christian ancestors all seem to have believed in some big picture with a God or gods and some form of afterlife. Were they right after all? Even in the Western world, there many variations concerning where we came from and what happens to us after death. Most religions believe in some sort of heaven and hell. Many believe that you are rewarded or punished according to your beliefs or conduct in this world. (Christianity, Judaism and Islam think along those lines today.) A soul, though, is essential in all these scenarios.

Other, non-western, religions also believe in some sort of soul and life beyond this earth. Buddhists believe in reincarnation, living many lives and learning lessons until perfection is reached. Hindus believe that all souls are part of a universal soul (Atman). After enough reincarnations one can become one with this soul, which is the sum of all the gods and the force which links everyone and everything together. Some believe at that point you become one with the universe. There are many variations and they vary in the precise mechanism of immortality. They agree on the notion that there is a bigger picture than the mortal earth, and that we are more than our earthly bodies. Many do believe that we were created, not a random happening. Called by many different names, these concepts have been generally around in some form or other since civilization began.

Where can we find the essential truth in all of this?

What is striking are the similarities between these concepts rather than the differences. Differences often seem to be cultural rather than fundamental. They all assume a creator or a universal force. They all assume a soul. They have a strong belief in everlasting life in some form. Where did these ideas come from? How did they spread, and how did they come to dominate our cultures? Can they all be wrong?

Where did religious belief come from?

It is interesting to look at where the concepts of religious belief originated from. Long before Christianity, our ancestors worshipped gods of all kinds. Indeed Christianity can be seen to be built on some shared ideals and principles that pre-existed in other sects, such as the Essenes or indeed mainstream Judaism. These religions were themselves influenced by older ideas and sects. The concept of a higher being, or beings, set above the earthly mortal man, seems to have been with us almost since thinking began.

My personal conventional religion, Christianity, which is mainstream to our society, has been around for more than two thousand years. Organized religion in general has been around for many thousands of years before that. The one God (monotheism) preached by Jesus and the prophets of the Old Testament replaced the many gods (polytheism) of the Roman empire in the western world. Islam also worships one God.

Why do people need religious beliefs?

Where could this need to have belief have come from? The answer is that it seems to be embedded in our culture. But why should this be so? It can be understood that our ancient ancestors needed the idea of God or gods as a survival mechanism. When life seemed brutal, dangerous and arbitrary, it was comforting to look for an outside reason for things that were happening. If good and bad events could be seen to be directed by an outside force, then that force could perhaps be placated by worship or ritual and sacrifices. A bad harvest could mean mass starvation. When family and friends die prematurely, it is human nature to look for a bigger picture, and comforting to believe that life goes on in some form. Is it just a human need to feel that there is a big picture, that life is not just random? Atheists would probably say that that was what religion is all about, no more. Could that be all there is to it?

Genetic advantage

Well, there is, of course, the view that this need for a higher power, or a big picture, is only in our genes, and not based on reality at all. It may have helped survival in primitive times. You could better cope with disaster if you thought there was a bigger picture and it was not all random. Belief that God was on your side would make you more confident and stronger. Belief in afterlife could help you to cope with the loss of a loved one more easily. You would behave better towards your fellow man, to the advantage of society in general, if there was the concept of being judged by your actions and punished or rewarded in an afterlife. Could this instinct towards religion have developed purely because it was a genetic advantage for early survival? Has it been hardwired in to the brain? By chance or by design? Or did these ancients actually understand things which we have forgotten?

The idea of God or gods, and life continuing after death, would probably not have had such a strong grip on the human mind over so many thousands of years if it was just based on this fear of the unknown. The religious myths would not have spread and taken root in our culture had there not been an idea in our subconscious that physical life on earth was not all there was.

Communication with other realms

On a more practical note, there have always been people through-out the millennia of earth's existence, who have seemingly been able to communicate with powers other than those that are merely earthly. Prophets, priests, seers, oracles and even wise men of all cultures, have been taken very seriously throughout our civilization, by the educated as well as the ignorant. Some would say, from where else, other than from a higher power, could they have received their information and guidance?

For instance, in religious circles these messages to us about the nature of our souls, and the world around us, were brought to us by prophets. As well as the teachings by Jesus, there are many other insights, concerning God and his creations, documented in the Old Testament of our Bible. Similarly, the insights of Mohammed and Buddha, and many others, are documented in their culture's religious historical documents. More recently, Joseph Smith, founder of the Church of Latter Day Saints (the Mormons) is considered a prophet by his followers. Prophets are supposed to be divinely inspired and given messages and guidance, from a higher power, to convey to us all. Joseph Smith received his guidance and teachings from an angel. Angels are considered God's messengers. They are also spoken about in many non-religious contexts though.

Can we believe the written word?

We have written records of the wisdom and works of the prophets and seers and their revelations in our Bible, and other holy books. But it does have to be asked, how accurate are they? Can we take them to be true? Do they give a true record of what was said and done at the time? On one hand, these can be powerful sources of clues in our search for the truth about reality. On the other hand, we must remember, however, that the words of the prophets or religious leaders would have been interpreted according to the cultural norms of the day. For instance, the Holy Bible, originally compiled around 60 A.D., was later heavily edited in the fourth century A.D. by the Roman Emperor Constantine. It is known that parts that he did not like or agree with were left out. Most importantly it was written with the cultural slant of a male-dominated society structured by the Roman empire. Women, said to have an equal role as preachers and teachers in the early church, were now dismissed and suppressed. Also, recent evidence and finds in the middle east have shown that there were actually around forty Gospels, all written many years after the events portrayed. Most of these were suppressed or lost if they did not support the 'party line' at the time. Interestingly, I am told that the Koran in Islam can be interpreted to give equal status to women and men. This was, and is, also seemingly negated by the laws and culture of the time. It is also suggested in some circles that the original Christian teaching on reincarnation has been heavily supressed. This is a contentious area with powerful arguments from scholars on both sides.

Mixed messages

We may never know the whole truth. The point is that in all long-standing religions, the original message is often overlaid with layers of interpretation of the cultural norms of the time. It is often very difficult to distinguish between the actual spiritual, or practical, message and an unwittingly biased interpretation by the powers that be, when it was written. Any challenge to organized religion is not necessarily challenging its idea of God, or of his existence. Rather, it is challenging man-made, culturally-biased ideas which may or may not have been the true interpretation of the original message, but have now been mixed up with it, as if they were. These things are often mixed up together, preventing objective study of what actually happened. This makes gleaning the truth of things from the written records of the time very difficult.

Take the Christian religion: The Council of Nicaea was instigated by Emperor Constantine, a Roman Emperor, to decide on how the Church was structured in the 4th century A.D. It was also to try and settle questions such as the true nature of Christ. For many centuries priests were debating whether he was a man doing the creator's work, a god seeming to take human form, or part of a trinity of Father, Son and Holy Ghost. It was the latter that was decided on, although it was a vicious bone of contention for years. Yet at school and in church we are taught these matters of opinion as fact, and irrefutable fact at that. That is not to say that they were wrong, just that at this distance it is just not possible to know. It is worth repeating here that, the underlying message of Christianity, however, is a good and useful road map to live life by.

Thus, we have no physical proof that the earthly domain is not all there is to life. On the other hand though, over the centuries many strange things have happened to people that could only be explained if the physical world were not the whole story. Some of these phenomena, such as healing, I will look at in later chapters. Also, there is little actual proof, other than strong human instincts and the testimony of prophets and seers over the millennia, that the god that we have been told made us, and our soul, actually exists. That is why believing in god as our creator is called faith. Faith is believing without physical proof.

The watchmaker analogy

There is one argument that is used to 'prove' the existence of a God, or designer, that has some value. It is called the watchmaker analogy. If you were walking in an uninhabited desert and saw on the ground a beautiful watch you would know that somewhere there is a watchmaker. The planet earth and the human race are such a beautiful complex harmonious construct, like a complicated watch, that they must have been constructed. Therefore somewhere there must be a constructor of humanity. Whether it is the conventional God or not is another matter.

The alternatives

Is the idea of a benevolent creator likely? What are the alternatives? There are those who believe that we are designed by a non-conventionally religious designer of some sort. The possible nature of this designer is even less clear than are the theories surrounding the conventional religious options.

Notwithstanding all this, the concept of a soul, a consciousness above and beyond our biological being, is almost certainly valid. It could not have existed so strongly in our society, hard-wired into our genes or not, if there was not a wealth of anecdotal evidence and experience to support it over the years. The notion of heaven and hell as described by mainstream religion, however, is questionable to say the least. The principle of life after death is worth hanging on to. The history of mainstream religion does provide some anecdotal evidence for continued existence beyond death. Millions and millions of people, from learned intellectuals to peasants tilling the fields, cannot have all been completely wrong.

To sum up, as mentioned before, I eventually rejected organized religion as many of us do. It felt stifling and illogical. As usually happens, in rejecting organized religion, the concept of a soul, and a continued existence after death, was also rejected. It was only after many years of thinking and reflecting that I realized that this may have been a mistake. The extra soul/essence above and beyond the biological brain can be shown to exist with or without the guardianship of organized religion. That can be shown to be reality. Near Death and Out of Body Experiences, amongst other phenomena, indicate this possibility. There is simply an overwhelming amount of transcultural and anecdotal, and even some scientific, evidence that a soul of some sort does exist.

Can we reject religion out of hand? Not necessarily; the existence of a possible mechanism for continuation after physical death may be the one thing which gives some credence to the mainstream Christian beliefs that I was brought up with. Also, heaven and hell could exist in some of the other, unseen, dimensions, that science is now understanding may be around us. The more difficult, and probably unanswerable, questions are, though, if that creator god actually exists, what form does he/she take, and what are the alternative scenarios if he does not?

The concepts of good and evil

There are other matters which may shed some light on the probability of the existence of God though. For instance, bound up with this belief, are the concepts of good and evil. If good and evil can be shown to exist, beyond the mere biological entities that are mankind, then that may indicate that the concept of a traditional supreme being cannot be so easily dismissed. Understanding of these concepts and their role in our society, may anyway give us more clues to the actual nature of reality. The problem of course is in the human definition of these concepts.

Good

What is good? We almost always know it when we see it, but it is harder to define than you would think. My dictionary defines good as "possessing and displaying moral virtue". Other definitions I can find range from morally positive, unselfish, law abiding (although what happens if the laws of your society are bad?), to being kind and caring towards others. Following God's laws, which have been set down by the commandments as rules to live by, for some people would be the main criterion. God, we are told, is pure goodness. We all know of people that are intrinsically good, without always being able to put into words why we feel that way.

Evil

Evil, strangely, seems slightly easier to define. It can be defined as morally negative, not living by God's rules. Putting your own needs above others. Some acts which can be seen as evil can actually be a result of extreme selfishness. People take what they want, swindle or steal, or invade or even kill or torture others because they feel that their needs and pleasures are more important than those around them. Some may do these things deliberately, or evilly. Others may be unaware or unconcerned of the effect of their actions on others. Their intentions are not evil, although the result of their actions can be considered so. Is this real evil, or just a malfunction of their 'survival of the fittest' biological genes? Some people do seemingly evil acts because they are mentally ill. We have all heard of those poor individuals who kill strangers in the grip of a delusion. They are ill rather than evil. Evil, it seems, requires malice. It requires a deliberate intention to do harm, even at the expense of others.

Tales of the Devil

If evil does exist, who is said to encourage and help facilitate it? Biblically, or historically, the candidate is, of course, the devil. Although a surprising number of people seem to feel that there may be a force of evil throughout the world, not everyone thinks that it has a physical face. The devil is traditionally the tempter to sin or evil. He has also been known as Satan, Lucifer and Beelzebub. He is seen as luring humanity away from good, to a path of evil. His role is to tempt us all to sin, and encourage us not to follow God's laws. There are also those who claim to use supernatural powers derived from him, to enable them to dominate others or commit evil acts. This includes so-called black magic. Literature abounds with stories of good versus evil. Some believe that we are in a constant battle to ensure that the forces of good are not overwhelmed by the forces of evil.

Others feel that the devil is only a symbol of evil. His physical form was imagined by painters and church men of old, and became set in our consciousness as he was then portrayed. He was imagined as half man, half beast, almost in the style of some gods of the ancients. He is often portrayed with horns and a tail, often red in the face. I have spoken to churchmen who believe that he does not exist on this plane, any more than God does, but uses agents. These are demons. I am told that in the Christian church there is a range of opinion even to his actual existence. There are those who believe in the hell fire version as stated in parts of the Bible, and those who are backing away from the concept.

The difficult questions

The key questions are then, if evil exists, is it just part of being human, almost an extreme of self-centredness, or is it something more? Is there an agency or a being that encourages perpetration of these so-called evil acts, for its, or their own ends? Are good and evil man-made concepts, developed to quantify and thus help regulate human behaviour? Is the devil just a symbol, or excuse for some bad behaviour? Or do the concepts of good and evil and the devil actually reflect a greater, God-created, reality?

Another great debate seems to be, not whether evil actually exists, however you define it, but surprisingly, whether it is a necessary counterpart to good? Are good and evil one system or two? If God is an all-powerful creator why does he allow evil to exist? Is it deliberate on some level? Are there the two great opposing powers fighting for the soul of humanity, or is evil a tool used by God to allow us to develop, grow and change? Is the devil leader of the opposition? Is he created by, or equal to God? Evil, or its temptations, can be seen, as I found in a quotation on the internet from Martin Buber, as "…the yeast in the dough". That is, the ferment placed in the soul by God to allow it to be grown and tested. "We can be tested as souls by our use or refusal of evil ways." This debate has strong adherents on both sides.

Proof of outside forces at work

Is there any proof of forces of good and evil in the world? I have not personally seriously encountered either. Do evil spirits exist? Are the forces of good ever openly seen? There is a vast literature, and a wealth of anecdotal evidence to support people's direct experience of both. I have spoken to people who feel they have encountered evil. I do not doubt that it exists. The Christian church does after all have a deliverance mission, which among other things, casts out evil spirits. Also, there is a service of exorcism which can be and is performed from time to time. What does the existence of both say about a possible big picture beyond earth?

There are those who feel they have experienced evil, there are those who feel they have been in the presence of absolute good. I personally have not experienced either, although I have spoken to people who have felt that voices have tried to tempt them onto a dark path. I have also encountered very selfish people, who have wreaked havoc on others lives. They could not in all faith be considered evil though. However, the conventionally religious story cannot be completely dismissed out of hand.

Heaven and Hell

Is heaven (resting place for souls of the good) and hell (place of torture for the evil/bad) likely? No one has come back from either with hard evidence, although some claim to have received messages from souls now in the heavenly fields. Both places are considered outside of visible creation, so unverifiable. All we can know, though, is that science is moving towards the concepts of a multidimensional universe, so anything is possible.

Aspects of reality

*   If you accept that there is the evidence for our continuing conscious -ness beyond death, then there may be a case for a religious soul.

*   If you accept the evidence of the watchmaker analogy also, then the case for a designer strengthens.

*   This designer may be the conventional God of our upbringing, or something quite different that we cannot yet imagine.

*   Some say that the need for religion may be just a survival instinct hardwired into our genes.

*   If you accept the case for the existence of good and evil, therefore God and the devil, the possibility for the scenarios as outlined in our Christian Bible becomes more possible.

*   Heaven and hell may exist in a multidimensional universe.

*   Clues to a bigger picture are to be found written in holy books, but time and cultural filters may have distorted them.

*   There have always been those who have communicated with other realms. This does indicate that there may be other realms that are available to communicate with.

The only definite conclusion we can draw at the moment, is that the world around us is more complex than science will allow, but not necessarily as religion states it to be. There seems to be another dimension to our lives, other than the physical world about us, that we cannot see. We must look at other clues, or reflections of reality, to try and make more sense of the grand scheme of things. All we can know is that this physical, biological life on earth is not the whole story. Conventional religious thought may be just a distorted reflection of an absolute, unknowable, ultimate reality.

CHAPTER FIVE

Angels and other entities

In my research, the next question I asked myself was: what other clues
to a more complex reality, beyond that which we can easily see, can
be found in our earthly realm? The answer is that it seems we are not,
whatever the powers that be say, really alone. Our reality seems to be
shared, at least according to some people, by other entities or beings,
luckily usually here to help humanity. It is in looking at these beings
that we get glimpses, or reflections, of other greater realities beyond
our earth. These helpers include angels and nature spirits.

Angels

In the last chapter I looked at the Christian Bible for some clues
as to the truth of things. Although the information given there may
not be totally accurate, there is an interesting otherworldly class of
beings that the Holy books assume exist. These are called angels, and
they have always been a mainstream part of conventional religion.
They seem also almost routinely accepted and talked about in much
of our esoteric, non-conventionally spiritual movements. They are
also the stuff of legends in many worldwide cultures. Can they be
proven to actually exist in our world? If this is so, what could this
indicate about the nature of the overall big picture of life?

In the western world, many of us of a spiritual or religious bent,
were brought up with the concept of the reality of angels. Indeed it was
reinforced weekly through the church and teachings in school. A belief
in their existence is almost mainstream in our society and culture.

What exactly are angels?

They are said to be beings of light that sometimes take a physical form. They are different from the ghosts and other spirits that we may also come across in literature, and will look at later. Angels are considered to be of non-human, or even divine origin. They are often portrayed as winged messengers from God in the Bible. The word angel itself is said to be derived from the Greek word *angelos* meaning messenger. Conversely they are considered in some circles to be inter-dimensional beings. Whatever the truth they are prominent in Islam, Christianity and Judaism. Indeed these religions actually share some of the same angels. They are also considered to be very real in most 'alternative' philosophies. Healers and clairvoyants sometimes claim to be guided by them, or use them in healing. They are mostly invisible to our human eyes, but can often, I am told, be felt as a comforting presence.

Some people also believe that angels have warned them of imminent danger. They often pop up in our Bible stories and were much discussed by the religious figures in our lives. I happened to go to a Catholic school, and to the nuns and priests they were very real. The most famous example is perhaps the Bible story about the angel visiting Mary to tell her that she would give birth to baby Jesus. On his birth also, the heavens were supposed to be filled with a multitude of angels (St Luke's gospel). They are spoken about throughout the New and Old Testament of the Bible and the Koran, instructing and exhorting and informing the characters at critical moments. There are even supposed to be some bad, or fallen angels who, having been thrown out of paradise, do the work of the devil.

Some of us were even brought up with tales of a personal guardian angel. Every person has, the theory goes, an individual angel allocated to them, who is there to guard and protect them, for life. Some alternative practitioners also claim to see them, or work with them to heal or guide. Friends of mine actually work with angels for healing and guidance in their lives. They are actually felt to be available to all who need them and not just to those of religious bent.

What do angels look like?

We imagine them, if we think about it at all, as the figures portrayed in the holy paintings of the middle ages. We do not know where these painters got their information that this was how they looked; there is not, I believe, a definitive actual description of their physical appearance in the Bible. These original images persist in our minds as fact today.

Artists and religious illustrators seem to portray them with long flowing white garments and large feathered wings Angels, in keeping with the male dominated culture of Biblical times, are assumed to be male. Sometimes, at crucial times, they are said to take the form of human beings. Islam, as I understand things, regards them as beings of pure energy, which are invisible, neither male nor female. Their mission is primarily is to praise Allah. Although there is, I understand, at least one description in Islamic lore of Archangel Michael. He is portrayed with wings of emerald green covered in saffron hairs. Some modern observers of angels report seeing just beings of light, without concrete physical form. My angel practitioner friends tend to see them as pure energy fields who will take some physical form if required.

Proof of their existence

Do angels actually exist? Or are they figments of the ancients (and our) imagination? I was certainly doubtful of their existence as a child. Yet to the nuns and priests who taught me, they were very real.

Can their existence be scientifically proven? As we are, after all, nothing but vibrating energy in a vast electrical field, anything may be a possibility. Actual proof might be difficult, but it is only our modern culture that seems to think if something cannot be proven to exist scientifically, it cannot possibly be real. There is a wealth of ancient and modern anecdotal evidence that some sort of beings as described have always existed, and helped individuals or groups of people. Angels have been talked about throughout history. There is simply too much written and spoken testimony for the concept of angels to be dismissed out of hand. Not only are they a constant in the Holy books; 'new age' books and the internet are also filled with stories of modern angel sightings and angelic intervention. As with anything slightly strange, though, people who have had such interactions often fear ridicule, and tend to keep quiet about it in general company.

As mentioned before, the Mormon religion was formed in 1820 when an angel called Moroni appeared to guide Joseph Smith. This angel was, however, said to have once been human. This is another interesting variation on the theme.

Physical witness

More recently, in 1985 Soviet Cosmonauts, orbiting earth in Salut 7, are reported to have seen 'seven giant figures in the form of humans but with wings and mist-like halos as in the classic description of angels'. They saw this group on more than one occasion. The Hubble Telescope has also been reported to have had strange sightings which have been hushed up. Is this likely? One would hope not, but it has to be said that there have always been suspicions that the mainstream scientific community would suppress those things which did not fit in with what it felt to be scientifically possible.

It has to be asked though, why do different people seeing angels, report seeing different things? It is interesting to note that people reporting such sightings tend to see what they expect to see. What is going on here? Those of us brought up in the western tradition of angels as white-robed, winged creatures see generally white-robed, winged creatures. Those brought up in different cultures, or from different eras, see whatever the general perception of angels or spirits are supposed to look like. Also as mentioned before, some people twho claim an angelic visit report just seeing a glowing light energy. Does this mean that it is all in our imaginations? Not necessarily. There are several factors that could be at work here which we will talk about later. Put briefly, if angels do exist and are advanced beings it is quite logical that they would appear to humans in a form that they would recognize and understand. What we can see is limited by our sense organs and the way our brain synthesizes the information it receives from them.

Have I seen an angel personally? The answer happens to be no, but I have spoken to many, quite sensible, ordinary people, not necessarily conventionally religious, who have reported some form of sighting or encounter. I have, however, come to believe that such beings do exist; what they actually are, though, is another matter.

The view of science

Would either the religious or alternative view of angels be scientifically possible? Well, we are energy beings at base. I do not expect most scientists would say their existence is provable, though. Are other unseen dimensions around us from which they may originate a possibility? Strangely, yes. There are many advanced theories in the world of cosmology and physics which indicate that such dimensions are both possible and likely.

Angels do appear to be assisting the human race in some way. Why? What does that indicate in any big picture of the universe? If such beings as angels do actually exist, what does that say about our reflections of our aspects of reality?

Aspects of angelic reality

• They are inter-dimensional beings. This could be possible, as physics is now working with the concept of a multi-dimensional universe. If that is what they are, an important question has to be asked. This is, why would beings from another dimension be interested in helping mankind?

• They are helpers sent from a creator. The answer to this question is a matter of faith. We were certainly brought up to think so. The creator may not be our conventional religious God, though.

• Perhaps they are creatures of the earth as we are. Just a different and more advanced type of natural being. Are beings made of pure energy a possibility? That is, at present, unknowable.

• If they are none of the above, then it gets really interesting. From what reality could they actually come? Are there multi layers of reality around and above us that we cannot see? Until we really know the big picture, this is also unknowable.

All we can say for sure when discussing angels is that their very existence is a big clue that the reality that we have been taught exists is nowhere near the whole story. They are reflections from a greater reality, not fully understood by us at the moment.

Nature spirits

There is another class of beings which seemingly help both nature and the human race. They are not as generally talked about and accepted as angels are, but are considered vital by some for our very existence. I refer to the so-called devas and other nature spirits that are said to exist in all growing things on the earth.

The theory goes that every growing thing has an invisible (to most) etheric helper. Their purpose seems to be to help the plants of our biosphere grow and thrive. Nature simply would not function without them.

What could they be? The Theosophists, I am told, believe them to be part of a separate branch of evolution. Others believe that they are part of the angelic kingdom, involved from the beginnings of time in the very creation of the earth. The theory is that evolution, as described by Charles Darwin, could not have succeeded without their help. There are supposed to be many different types, including the elementals residing in earth, air, fire and water. Some consider that the gnomes, fairies, giants and others of our mythology were actually manifestations of these nature spirits. All have different jobs to do.

What do they look like?

Most people have not the ability to see them; those that have done so just refer to energy glows. Some feel them, some people claim that they are just able to know that they are there and are able to work with them. Of course they probably do not look like the pictures in our children's story books. I have spoken to a couple of very sensitive people who claim to have seen them. They claim that they have seen fairies. These apparently are just buzzy flashes of energy, vibrating so quickly that there is some sort of impression of wings. These devas are supposed range in size from one atom to unimaginably large.

They are all considered to be essential for the continuation of life on earth. Some people believe that the earth itself is a vast nature spirit, known as Gaia.

Proof

Apart from the personal experience of many people, there is, of course, no scientific proof that these spirits exist. There is some confirmation, though, in the existence of the Findhorn Foundation in Scotland. Their claim is that they use the nature spirits to wrest abundant crops out of fundamentally inhospitable ground. They have done so very successfully for many years. The principle is to work co-operatively and co-create with nature.

Is the existence of these beings likely? I have certainly never come across one. Although their reality is unprovable with our limited science, in practice, again, there is considerable anecdotal evidence across many cultures. The possibility of their existence cannot be completely ruled out. Some people do believe that angels are themselves just a particular kind of deva.

Aspects of reality

- Whatever the exact truth of the reality of these angels, devas and elementals, there do seem to be, usually unseen, entities operating alongside humanity.

- Where they actually come from and why they are helping us is a mystery.

- The only thing we can be sure of is that life and reality on earth is many layered, and probably multi-dimensional and not necessarily just as we perceive it to be.

Whether you believe they exist or not, the reality of the existence of angels and elemental spirits may be beyond the experience or imagination of most ordinary people. But alongside these entities operating in our reality, there seem to be other disembodied spirits. I refer, of course to the phenomenon of ghosts. There is also the matter of the spirits of the dead that seem to be able to communicate with those left behind. It is to these classes of beings that I turn my attention in the next chapter.

CHAPTER SIX

Ghosts and other spirits

Glimpses of these other entities that seem to be sharing our world do give more insights, more reflections, of possible ultimate universal realities. Importantly, the existence of other, unseen, dimensions around us for them to operate from are hinted at. This concept is scientifically more mainstream than you may imagine. Science is moving towards the possibility of a multi-dimensional universe. The possible proof of the existence of these dimensions, and also evidence for the continuation of the human spirit after death, can also be reflected in the existence of the slightly different class of more earthly spirit entities. In this chapter I look at these strange phenomena. I mean, of course, those of ghosts and other spirits, and the possibility of communication with the spirits of those physically dead.

Communication with the dead

Alongside what we think of as conventional religious thought, there are other institutions and people in our society that assume continuation after death is self-evident. It is understood by them that life does go on in some, usually spirit, form. This belief happens both on an individual and an organized level. The general belief seems to be that on leaving the physical body the soul/essence moves to a higher plane somewhere beyond our physical universe. Communication between those of us still on the earthly plane and those departed is thought possible. It is in these communications that the proof of our continuation beyond death, and a multi-layered universe exists. There are several different ways that people do this.

Spiritualism

This is a worldwide movement which has strong roots in the UK and America. It has this as its guiding principle: that life after death exists. It can be proved to do so by adherents communicating with the spirits of the dead. This is now a quasi-mainstream and respectable institution. Every big town, and many small ones, have Spiritualist Churches. My own town of Poole has at least two. Some indeed see no conflict between Christian principles and Spiritualism and call themselves Christian Spiritualists. The belief is that there is a creative force in the universe which some of them know as God. The main premise is that the created universe has many unseen dimensions. It is also believed that when we die, our spirit part, or our soul, moves over to the next dimension above. If the departed want to they can then communicate back to living loved ones and help and guide them. The physical body may return to its constituent parts but the spirit/soul energy cannot be destroyed and must remain in some form.

I am told that Spiritualism has the following 7 principles:
1. The fatherhood of God, the divine source.
2. The brotherhood of man.
3. The communion of Spirits and the Ministry of Angels.
4. The continuous existence of the human soul.
5. Personal responsibility.
6. Compensation and retribution hereafter for all the good or evil done on earth. (I understand that to be some form of Karma, possibly occurring over several lives rather than in heaven or hell)
7. Eternal progress open to every soul.

If they are Christian Spiritualists there is also an additional principle, which is a belief in the leadership of Jesus Christ.

All spiritualists do believe that the departed spirits exist unseen around us. Our physical body may have gone, but our essence or soul is intact after death. The departed souls of our loved ones are presumed to be still around us. They are watching us as we live our physical lives. They may take an interest in those that they had an emotional or family connection with, when they were alive.

Evidence for continuation after death

Spiritualists seek to prove this continuance by holding services in their spiritualist churches. These often, like more conventional churches, may involve both hymns and some form of prayer. Unlike mainstream churches, however, they may also feature clairvoyance from the platform. This is to demonstrate that life does go on beyond death. Messages are received and channelled through so-called mediums for members of the congregation. Healing is often also done for those who need it.

I myself visited a local Christian Spiritualist church and witnessed this demonstration of clairvoyance. Those receiving the messages felt that they were accurate and seemed to feel that it was indeed proof that their loved ones had continued after death in some form.

Mediumship

Many people, even beyond this organized Spiritualism, also believe they have individual direct access to this spirit world and work as mediums. Some work via the Spiritualist churches, some work alone. Mediums, as the name would indicate, act as intermediaries. They have gifts which enable them to see and hear what most people cannot. Many claim to have seen spirits from the time of their childhood. All claim to receive messages from departed souls to reassure loved ones left behind. They say that this is both to prove that life goes on, and to warn and guide those left behind. The thinking is that it is the nature of things that people will suffer through life. Loved ones will die, people will make wrong choices and some will fall on hard or difficult times. With spirit guidance people can lessen grief by understanding that their loved ones do go on in some form. People can also be warned if a future action is not in their best interests. It is worth remembering though that there may be errors in transmission and interpretation of messages. It is also to be remembered that those departed souls are only 'human' and are not omnipotent.

The process is not always straightforward. Some mediums have greater gifts than others. Some departed souls are better at communicating with mediums than others. Some employ so-called spirit guides to help them facilitate communications. These can be anyone who has taken on the task from the 'other side'. The helpers may include old friends, wise people from our own or different cultures, or even animals. Some mediums hear words and some claim to see visions. Some even seem to be temporarily taken over by the departed and speak with their voice.

Evidence of mediumship

It has to be asked, could some mediums be fooling people and making things up? There may be, as in every walk of life, unscrupulous people pretending to have these gifts to make money. They are usually quickly spotted and get a very bad reputation. If they are not accurate they will not be successful. In any field there are charlatans, it is unavoidable. There is, however, overwhelming anecdotal evidence from people's personal experience, that it is possible to communicate with departed spirits or souls. There has been much written about it. There is also some scientific proof. For instance, Gordon Smith, a famous Psychic medium, also known as the 'psychic barber' did (and passed) double blind trials for the Scottish Society for Psychical Research, based at the university of Glasgow. Personally, I have direct evidence. Attending an Aunt's funeral, I wore my late mother's earrings. I did this to represent her, as she and the Aunt had been very close when younger. My elder daughter knew nothing about this. She visited a medium for guidance and healing. She received a message from my mother, via the medium, which puzzled them both. She consulted me later as to what the message may have meant. It was, she said, something about wearing her (my mother's) earrings!

Some mediums also work in smaller groups in their homes where they can seemingly manifest other phenomena, such as table lifting and voices from beyond. This is done either through a medium or through a 'trumpet' receiver through which disembodied voices can be heard. Unfortunately there was much fakery and pretence in the early stages. But that does not change the fact that many respectable people practise or have firm belief in the phenomena. A friend of mine worked for many months with a private group, trying to communicate with the beyond. She has tapes of disembodied voices on which spirits can be clearly heard trying to communicate. The voices sound strange but they are actually on a tape, on record. It was not a group hallucination.

There are many cases also, some reported in the press, in literature or on the internet, of mediums or clairvoyants knowing personal information about their subjects which otherwise they would have no access too. Sometimes the information about the subject's family is unknown to the subject and has to be confirmed by another older family member. Another friend reported to me that her late father had visited her to accurately warn of her mother's impending passing over. He did this so that she would be prepared when it happened.

Both conventional religious beliefs and spiritualist churches and a great number of ordinary people are certain that our essences/souls continue in some form after physical death. Mediums do seem to channel communications between departed souls and those living, for their help and guidance. Sometimes they are not sure how it works but they just know that it does, and is real and often very accurate.

Possible mechanisms of spiritual continuation after death

The question has to be asked, of what reality is this communication with those departed a reflection? How does the phenomenon fit into the big picture of the universe? I asked a friend, who does work as a medium, what he thought may be the physical mechanism. He sent me a written explanation. It was so clear and useful that I have reproduced it, with his permission, almost word for word. The suggested mechanism actually refers back to our atomic structure. It involves the fact that we are beings made essentially of energy, as discussed at the beginning of my research.

Simon stated "*I believe that throughout the entire universe there is one energy or source. Our earth exists in this universe, therefore that energy flows through the earth and therefore through every thing and being that inhabits this earth. This is one of the many old tai chi beliefs, and is still believed by many old chi masters.*

All matter is made up of elements and atoms, which form different densities by vibration, the slower the vibration the denser the matter or forms of existence i.e. solid, liquid, gas etc. With this in mind, energy cannot be created or destroyed but can be transformed from one form to another. For example, kinetic energy to electrical energy to heat and light... e.g. turning on a light bulb.

It could follow that our soul's existence therefore also cannot be created or destroyed but does in fact go from one form to another, or from one life to another. It is becoming more acceptable to believe that the soul, or life-force, chooses its lessons and experiences in each lifetime, and when we have learned and experienced all that we are meant to, it's time to leave the present body and move on to the next soul mission; spiritualists call this 'karma'.

The soul life-force or being is energy on a higher vibration, this is why, I feel, mediums can communicate with different souls that have passed over to a different life or vibrational plain. Hence the physical and higher self!

We are similar to radios in that we can channel energy and translate it to understandable human language, so long as we believe we can tune in. This is possible because everything really is connected in some way or form, especially as nature doesn't like vacuums very much!

After all of the above is accepted, and we realize that all matter, be it physical or spiritual, is connected without gaps or spaces, then communication becomes instant and possible on many levels. Our soul cannot be created or destroyed, it just grows and develops as is planned.

We are part of one energy field."

Simon himself works a a medium and helps other people through his gifts. Not only are his words a possible explanation of continuation of life after death, they also give some possible explanation of mechanisms by which it may happen... This is a bigger and newer picture than we were taught at school or church, but it is just as logical, if not more so.

Is what he says possible? It may be very likely. We are after all just beings made of vibrating energy; even our thoughts seem to be made of bio-chemical electrical impulses. Some part of our mind, the part that is not necessarily just a function of our biological brain, does seem to go on and be part of a bigger universe that we cannot physically see. Whatever 'hard' science will say is possible or not possible, some people do seem to be able to communicate and receive guidance from those who have passed on. As we are all part of the same vast electromagnetic field this should be possible. Even in our own culture, which has moved further and further away from being religion dominated, there is overwhelming anecdotal evidence for a soul/essence or some part of us that passes on to a different realm; as there has been throughout our own history and the history of all other cultures and civilizations in the world.

There is also in Simon's explanation some indication of something generally undiscussed by our Christian religion, although taken as fact in most 'eastern' religions. I am referring of course to the possibility that we live more than once. The theory of reincarnation holds that our souls return to a different physical body many times, and do so for a purpose. I look at this theory more thoroughly in the next chapter.

Ghosts

The existence of ghosts is another strange thing that should not happen if the physical world was all there was. Ghosts usually seem to be some sort of versions, or copies, of people or objects that once lived in the 'real' world. There are many people that claim to have seen them or believe in their existence. They are another class of phenomena which can be seen as a visible proof of the continuation of our essence after death.

From almost the beginnings of recorded history, there have been stories of the appearance of these strange visitors from beyond the grave. I do not mean tales of our individual loved ones psychically communicating with us after death. This, as just discussed, sometimes does happen.

More general ghosts are a different matter. Their connection with mankind seems different from those souls communicated with by mediums. These more impersonal ghosts are often tied to a particular geographic location. Their very existence is another massive clue that life does continue in some form after death, and that the world we see is not the whole story.

Types of ghosts

Descriptions of these ghosts range from images that appear to be real people, often from a different historical time, to the classic headless horsemen or monks that seem to walk though solid walls. Some people report having heard sounds or just shapes. There are reports of the sound of footsteps when there is no one there, or sounds of children crying, among other phenomena.

There seem to be two broadly general types of ghosts. There are those that seem unaware of us in the 'real' world. They operate usually in a particular geographic location. They often repeat actions that they would have done when they were alive, for example, walk along paths that sometimes are no longer there, or walk around rooms that they once inhabited. Unlike the spirits that the mediums communicate with, they are often not aware that they are dead, or refuse to believe so. Some feel that most ghosts around us are actually not aware of us as people at all. They are just traces of people that have died and that have not moved on to the next phase of existence. They have become stuck and earthbound, locked into the place where they met their, often untimely end. This is usually because of some form of trauma.

There are also those ghosts that do seem to be in some way aware of us, and on some level communicate with us. There are those that are actually hostile. These may be referred to as poltergeists. Objects may be moved or thrown. There are many tales of these types of ghosts making ordinary people's lives difficult because of their actions. Sometimes thought to be feeding on the raw energy produced as a result of human emotions from a deep upset. Why do they act in that way? They may be unaware that they are dead and feel we are trespassing on their space. They may be also connected with darker forces that are part of a bigger picture.

Evil spirits

The Church of England even has a ministry (the Deliverance Ministry) that has been set up to release the spirits causing trouble to the earthly population. What does this all mean? What could the phenomena actually be? If the Church of England takes ghosts/spirits seriously, why does not the scientific establishment?

I have spoken to priests and spiritual healers about this problem of, so-called, evil spirits. There are mixed views concerning this topic. Although some cultures believe that it is possible for evil spirits to inhabit the bodies of innocent people, our culture is not so sure. The priest told me that he had often worked to release, not evil spirits but spirits of those who did not know they were dead or did not want to be dead. They 'took over' others' bodies to try and still exist in this world. He persuaded them to move onwards towards the light. The healer told me a similar stories and also added that disgruntled nature spirits also caused trouble for some people. Disturbed earth energies and elementals may cause physical objects to fly and doors to bang, as well as the departed trying to communicate with you. These are not ghosts, however, but something quite different.

Why ghosts?

The question has to be asked, if life does go on, as a soul or essence as described, in some type of electromagnetic energetic form, where does it go and why should it want to come back to earth? Or why should it be stuck on earth when it should have moved on? Why are we seeing images of the departed physical bodies still, long after the death and physical decay of these bodies? A big picture of an energetic continuum is hinted at here, but we cannot yet know the real picture.

Why do ghosts seem to manifest in a copy of their human physical body? There are three different possible explanations for this:

1. There is the question, that is discussed properly later, of the true nature of humanity and the origins of the human body. Scientific theory has it that as a species we evolved from primitive life forms,

through natural selection over the millennia to our current physical forms. As individuals we are the products of our parents' genes in combination and the form of our evolved species. Others say that it is too complex to have happened like that without a guiding hand. There is, however, a mind-blowing theory that, in fact, we, and all around us, evolved and became what we are because we all have energy or spiritual blueprints on which the physical body is based. We are born with this blueprint and grow to it. When we die, the outward physical body decays, but the energy of the blueprint can still be trapped in our dimension.

2. Ghosts are often seemingly unaware that they are dead. Can the soul/essence part of them that leaves the physical body be projecting what they think they still look like?

3. There is a theory that the trauma of dying violently, or unexpectedly, can cause the event or body to energetically imprint onto the surrounding area in which the event took place. It is known that more electrical impulses are released in periods of high drama or trauma, and these may have lingered on.

These explanations may appear strange but ghosts are a great anomaly in the conventional and scientific explanations on which our understanding of the world around us is based. Any or none of these may be true. All we can say is that there is substantial anecdotal evidence that ghosts do seem to exist; at least a great many people believe so. Some phenomena cannot just be explained away. There is also a theory that some levels of sound, that we are not consciously aware of, can trigger visual hallucinations. Even so, there seems to be a hard core of unexplainable ghost stories out there in our society.

Evidence for ghosts

Although there are always sceptics, the paper trail of written and verified ghost stories is quite impressive.

• Pliny the Younger wrote about Athenodorus's ghost in the first

Century AD. Pliny was a careful recorder of what he saw and heard. The philosopher Athenodorus allegedly went to Athens and looked for a home to rent. He found a cheap house with a very low rent because it was supposed to be haunted. Writing at his desk that very night he heard rattling chains and moaning. When he eventually looked up a filthy and thin old man, cruelly shackled stood before him. The ghost signalled Athenodorus to follow him and led him outside to a point in the garden. The next day the philosopher alerted the authorities who dug at the point indicated and found a skeleton of a shackled man. Once this had been properly buried the hauntings and bad luck ceased.[2]

• Our own Tower of London is said to be haunted by, among others, Anne Boleyn. She was executed there by her husband Henry VIII.

• Many castles and old houses have their resident ghosts. There are many stories told in books and on the internet, and many organizations dedicated to tracking and recording such things.

• There was a programme on television recently about ghosts on the London underground. It involved strange tales of ghosts in deserted tunnels, passengers walking through walls and footsteps and footprints appearing when there was no one there. These were all reported by burly railway men, who preceded almost every description with the statement that they did not believe in ghosts but this and this had happened to them. Often they had concealed the event from their fellow workers for fear of being labelled daft. Several independently described the same phenomena without being aware that others had witnessed the same thing.

• My local café in Blandford, 'The George', has a history of hauntings and strange unexplained phenomena. This includes manifestations of pockets of extreme coldness. Researchers have allegedly contacted a spirit, among others, of a small child that died falling down a well which has long since been filled in.

---

2   Yvette Fielding and Ciaron O'Keeffe.
     Ghost Hunters: A guide to investigating the paranormal.

Personal experience

Do I have any personal experience of ghosts or the supernatural? The answer is that I have not seen any ghosts, but that I have certainly encountered some strange phenomena.

• When touring in Wales, we booked into a hotel that we happened to drive past in Brecon. It was called the Castle Hotel. The site it occupied had been in use as some form of habitation for a thousand odd years. It was in a commanding position on a hill overlooking the river. A castle had been on the site for many years, and parts of the castle had been incorporated into the present day hotel. I casually asked the owner if it was haunted and he laughed. He told me he had a ballroom which is covered by CCTV. This had shown orbs of light manifesting on a nightly basis, like a firework display, he said. My husband and I walked down to the door of the ballroom when night fell. It was locked with a small padlock, with an inch or so gap between the doors. We saw no orbs but we felt and heard an enormous wind howling and rushing around. We could feel it, on our faces rushing out between the gap in the doors. We presumed it had come from outside (it was a filthy night), but a return visit in the morning light showed no mechanism by which it could have happened. This felt strange and scary; what could have been going on? We were not expecting the phenomenon (we were hoping for orbs) and we both felt it.

• Later that trip, also by chance, we found the oldest pub in Wales: The Skirrid Mountain Inn. This also turned out to be haunted. Conversation with the landlord revealed that above the bar the rooms were a court in olden days, with holding cells. (These were now tasteful bathrooms!) Over 100 people had actually been hanged on the premises. Rope marks were still showing on the staircase beams. The landlord told us that guests had often complained of feeling a noose tightening around their necks. Lots of other ghostly activity had been reported, and serious paranormal investigators were taking great interest in the premises. The most interesting statement that he made, though, concerned his small grandchild. This boy had come on a recent visit. It had been concealed from him that the place was supposedly haunted, so not as to scare him. He was sent to the toilet but refused to go in because "there was a strange man in a frock that would not let him in". The grandfather could not see the ghost, but the child could. The child did not know that the ghost was there, and that you should not be able to see people once they were dead.

These are both very old buildings with sometime violent histories, but in both of them ghosts were both expected and experienced. When discussing with friends, almost everyone has a ghost story, or knows someone that does. The evidence is out there if we choose to look.

A straw poll of friends reveals lots of small stories of unexplained footsteps, doors opening and closing, strange unexplainable lights and shadows that had no possible physical explanation. On asking a friend's father (D) if he had ever seen anything strange in his old cottage, he said "I saw someone from the past walking down the corridor the other day, but of course it was only my imagination I suppose". Another friend has a problem with a haunted kitchen. Saucepans routinely, and scarily, move up from the hob towards the ceiling. This relatively modern house also has ghostly people mani-festing quite regularly. They are told that the house is on a portal, a junction between dimensions. The occupants have become quite used to this happening.

The stories go on and on. Some may be fanciful or products of an overheated imagination. But there are just too many to dismiss the whole phenomenon out of hand. It is very interesting that many people, such as D and the railway men, see things that they do not actually believe that they should see. This, then, cannot be blamed on an over-active imagination. Some people, in some form, seem to return to or linger on this earth after death. Where this form comes from, its true nature and where it/we go to after death is another matter.

Why do not we all see ghosts?

I have often spoken to people who have sometimes seen strange things, including ghosts, as they go about their ordinary, every day, affairs. Why can they see things that I cannot? It may be a subtle difference in their sense organs or their brains. It may be that their brains are more able to process what they can see. It is quite striking that small children often see things that they do not realize that they should not be seeing (including my own grandson). They then often seem to lose the ability when they get older. This tends to happen when they realize that most people do not see them, or are taught that they do not exist. Many of the people who claim to see spirits or ghosts report that they were actually beaten, reprimanded or ridiculed as children when they said something about them, so learned to keep quiet.

Why do not all dead people become ghosts? Why cannot we all see and hear the dead? There almost always seems to be a reason, usually trauma or unfinished business, for the ghosts to manifest. Perhaps many people do not feel the need to communicate with a loved one after death. Logically, that it does not happen in all cases, shows that there must, in all probability, be somewhere else for all other spirits, who leave their physical bodies after death to go to. This may be the conventional godly realm, or perhaps it may be just another place or dimension that we cannot yet see. This is, anyway, another strong proof that we are not just the purely physical beings that we seem to be.

Conclusion

The strong case for the existence of both spirits and ghosts and communication with the dead, is an indication of a big picture that conventional thinking has not yet taken on board. What could it all mean? What is out there that conventional religious thinking has not wholly identified? There is a huge body of people out there, spiritualists, mediums and others who have experience of ghosts or communicating with those departed, either positively or negatively. It becomes self-evident that the human spirit still exists in some form after physical death. Where could it actually go after death?

The scientific explanation of the mechanism, I believe, will one day come about. Simon's explanation of the possible mechanism is not far from some of the science that I look at later. The important thing is, even if only a small proportion of the reported 'hauntings' and communications from the departed are true, there are strong implications for the truth of what is actually happening in our reality. The case for a multi-dimensional universe becomes stronger and stronger. The case for some sort of life after death, a continuation beyond the physical body, becomes almost unanswerable. These are very interesting reflections of reality indeed.

Ghosts may just be energetic reflections of their old physical body. They may also be just resonances of the electrical energy of the physical body imprinted on to the physical earth at a time of trauma which precipitated their dying. They may also be souls that are not aware they are dead. Anyway, they seem to somehow share our reality with us, without being considered a real part of it. Why this happens we cannot wholly know. We can guess at how, but why is a great mystery. The ghosts that do interact with us negatively indicate a possibility of an even stranger big picture.

Where could it be that we go to after death? Religious thinking will say it is that is to God's heaven and hell, both outside of visible creation. All we can say is that there is somewhere from which the departed can communicate back to earth. Somewhere there are other dimensions or places within our reality that we cannot see. There also seems to be a transitional stage, in which some spirits get stuck. We are not totally lost on death; our soul/essence continues in a recognizable form somewhere. Priests, mediums, spiritualists, ghost hunters and a huge proportion of the general public believe this to be true. Many people also believe that we are able to communicate with these other realms. We do continue beyond death in some form, and the visible physical earth is not all that there is to our reality. These are the only firm conclusions we can be sure of.

Aspects of reality

- Life after death does seem to continue in some form.

- The physical earth is not all there is in our reality.

- We are energy beings, and sometimes the energy of the departed becomes trapped in the earthly realm.

- Some people have the ability to communicate with the spirits of the dead, therefore their essence or consciousness must exist intact somewhere.

- The case for a multi-dimensional universe is strengthened.

There is another interesting question that we have to ask ourselves in our quest to look behind the reflections of our physical world in our search for the truth of reality. That is, if we can show that we continue after physical death intact in some form, then have we inhabited physical bodies more than once? If we have, and can be shown to have lived more than once, then this puts a whole new complexion on our tentative big picture of existence. It would make it bigger and more mysterious than we have dreamed before. It is to the topic of reincarnation that I look next.

CHAPTER SEVEN

Past lives, past livings

When looking at all the reflections of ultimate reality that we are able to see, none are more intriguing than the realization that we may have lived more than once. Could this actually be possible? The evidence is very strong that human consciousness does go on after physical death. Could it be possible that the part of us that does go on after physical death could come back and inhabit different bodies though time? If so this would put a whole new perspective on our understanding of reality.

Although I grew up in an ordinary but loving home, I always felt that I had had other life experiences. This was strange, in retrospect, given that it was never mentioned as a possibility, or even considered as a theoretical option. It was just something I knew. The school I went to, being of a religious nature, would have considered this heresy. Today these things are sometimes discussed freely, but in those days for most of us it was an unheard of concept. Hard evidence of reincarnation is very difficult to find, but there is a substantial amount of evidence from other people's experience.

The religious view

What does religion say about this concept? Well, today in the Christian religion, reincarnation is not officially considered as an option. Although I do know that privately some priests believe it to be a strong possibility. The rumour has it that the teachings about it have been long ago suppressed. So much was historically withheld and suppressed by the church hierarchy, if it did not fit in with the standard line. If you remember, it is fact that in the early days of the church, many texts were burnt and gospels destroyed if they did not follow the hierarchy's agreed line. We may never know what the early official teachings were, if any, on the matter.

Even so, some traces remain. Many think that some Bible texts can be interpreted to mean that, for instance, the prophet Elijah and John the Baptist may have been the same person but born at different times. The idea of reincarnation was, anyway, in existence at the time that the scriptures were written, and I am told that there is no actual Bible. Mainstream Islam also seems to reject the concept of reincarnation. Whereas some Sufi groups do believe in it, in some form I am told. The denial of thepossibility of multiple lives has not always been true of other religions and cultures however.

The view of the ancients

Many ancient thinkers and philosophers took the concept of reincarnation very seriously. For instance, in ancient Greece the great philosopher Plato took it for granted that we all live many lives and even choose before birth what type of life we want to live. The concept was not new then, it was accepted mainstream belief for many different cultures. Interestingly the ancient Egyptians believed in resurrection not reincarnation. Many 'eastern' religions such as Buddhism and Hinduism, still accept reincarnation as the norm today. Also, many so-called new age believers and practitioners also believe strongly in reincarnation. As do many ordinary religious and non-religious individuals. Even today, many 'primitive' cultures still believe that we have spirits which are separate from our physical form and that can leap from body to body.

The purpose of reincarnation

If it does happen, then what would be the point of reincarnation? One theory is that we are supposed to go through life's learning, experiencing life at all levels, and improving our souls. Our essence or soul continues without interruption in one dimension or the other. (As per Simon's theory in the last chapter) Life is one continual stream. We are all supposed to experience birth, death and re-birth until we are developed enough to be able to leave the cycle. The main idea is that we live different lives and play different roles to learn what it is to be human. We are sometimes male, sometimes female, sometimes rich sometimes poor. Sometimes we are a soldier, sometimes we are an aggressor, sometimes victim. We try and play as many roles as possible to learn and grow. All past life lessons and experiences are stored on our eternal memories. We choose possible lives to enhance and expand our knowledge and understanding. Things done or not done in this life can affect the path of future lives.

Is any of this possible? Well, if our soul/essence is separate from our physical body then the concept is not necessarily out of the question. Consciousness could, in theory, leave one body and return into another after death. Without discussing now the questions of why this should happen, and where souls go between lives, the major question is does it actually happen? Could it be glimpses of a strange big reality, or could it be all a figment of overactive imaginations?

It is very hard to prove that we do live many times. All we can say is that in establishing a possible mechanism in the continuation of some vital part of us after physical death we cannot rule it out completely. As we are supposed to be born with no memory of past lives, it should be impossible to even come up with any evidence at all. In practice, however, there seem to be some traces of past lives sometimes bleeding through into our present ones. It is in these strange glimpses that we can find some anecdotal evidence in support of this aspect of reality.

Evidence

The general evidence today is, of course, word of mouth; people's personal experience. Yet again I find that if you ask even the most unlikely people if they believe in the phenomenon, time and time again they sheepishly mention that they have often thought this was a possibility. They often give examples of seeing familiar places that they could not have been to before, or meeting people that they feel they have met before, but could not have done in practice. There may be other explanations, of course, but there is just too much, albeit fragmented, evidence of it to dismiss out of hand. Many people now have even written books about their experiences of the phenomena. They have researched their fragmented memories of past lives and traced back to find the person they used to be, and the places that they inhabited.

Is there any scientific evidence? Obviously these seemingly abstract things are difficult to prove in the laboratory. The way past life memories are often retrieved is by using a specialist practitioner and putting the subject under hypnosis. The conscious mind is usually not aware of them. This sort of procedure can lay itself open to claims of chicanery by the scientific establishment. Mainstream scientists find it very dubious. One of the safer ways to try and verify the phenomenon, at the moment, is by the study of past life memories of children.

Evidence from children

Children between the ages of two and five often spontaneously talk about previous lives and experiences. Whole books have been written where past lives have been checked up on. Scars and health problems have been linked to past life traumas. There is a famous book by Dr. Ian Stevenson, *Children who remember previous lives,* that documents all of this. Tom Shroder's book *Old Souls* documents some of Stevenson's travels with stories from both the US and India. This includes many strange stories, of differing quality, but too many to ignore completely. He found multiple examples of partly-remembered, recent past lives among children of all races and creeds. Many seemed to have died prematurely or traumatically, leaving a sense of unfinished business. There are also many contemporary stories to be found on the internet.

There appears to be a particularly high concentration among those who have religious beliefs or cultures that accept reincarnation as the norm, for example, Druse. Among Druse children it was quite common for children with memories of a past life to re-visit their 'old' stamping grounds and link up with previous family. Often an on-going relationship between the old and new families would ensue. Is this all fiction or overheated imagination? Although strong, not all memories were complete or one hundred percent accurate on all details. All stories that Stevenson had taken seriously, though, did contain details that could not have been easily known to people if they had not been who they claimed to be. We are not 'supposed' to remember past lives, but it was as if fragments of these lives had bled through into the current consciousness of these children. These memories were either ignored or taken seriously depending on the beliefs of the parents.

I also recently came across a book that added substantially to the available evidence of past lives related by children. It was called *Soul Survivor: The Reincarnation of a World War II Fighter Pilot* by Bruce Leininger.

It is the story of Leininger's small son James. James had terrible nightmares from a very young age. Strange things that he said to explain his distress to them over a period of time gave his family clues to a possible past life as a fighter pilot. He seemed to be re-membering crashing in an airplane and being trapped, dying in the war. The father, Bruce, was very sceptical. He was a Catholic who did not believe in reincarnation at all. He was actually looking for ways to disprove James' story. Nevertheless he chased down all the clues, and eventually even managed to identify who James may have been in a previous life. Surprisingly, and clinchingly, James had wartime information that was correct, but not in the public domain. There is no way that he could have known it as a small child, unless it was from personal experience. The father really struggled with this, as it was against all he had been taught about reality. He eventually came to the conclusion though, that (and I paraphrase) if God had chosen to do this for his own purposes, who are we to argue.

There are examples also from friends and relations. For instance, an acquaintance of mine told me the story of her daughter, who as a very young child, executed perfect dance moves. She had not had lessons in, or access to dance. She used to comment, when surprise was shown at her abilities, that of course she used to be a dancer in Rome. She herself has now no conscious memories, of either Rome, or her dancing as a child. Also, my own grandson, James, as a very small child, ran into the road. When his mother told him off and said how awful it would be if he was killed, he nonchalantly remarked that she was not to worry as he would just come back as a baby again. He has, of course, completely forgotten this now. Small children are interesting studies as they tend to be totally disingenuous. They say what they say without the filter of what is acceptable or understandable in our society. They tell it as it is.

Adult evidence

From an adult perspective, Jenny Cockell wrote a book titled *Yesterday's Children* which documents her obsession with, and memories of, a place and children that she had dreamt about for many years. The mother of the family, whom she felt she had been, had died prematurely and was desperately worried about the fate of the children that she had left behind. It was years before she was able to try and check up on these 'memories' that had been haunting her. As before, they were not one hundred percent clear but she did eventually find the place that she had dreamt about but never actually visited. She, due to modern technology, was even able to find some of her 'children', who were able to confirm many details that she had dreamt about their childhood and no one else could have known to be true.

Personal experience

There is my own personal evidence. This was the feeling that, despite what I had been taught, I had lived before. This grew slowly. But when I met my first husband we both instantly, out of the blue, felt that we had met before, but not in this life. He came from a similar background to mine with a family that never dreamt of discussing such things. Indeed, as far as I knew they never even thought about the above and beyond at all. We both felt it very strongly, though. This was very strange. Later, and gradually, more clues bled though into my consciousness. Why did I understand things which should have been beyond my comprehension? Why was I afraid of sailing, although I loved the water and swimming? (I now 'know' that I have been trapped under a boat and drowned). Why did I always feel that

I had done so many things before? It was years later that I began to understand the possible mechanisms, but the feelings were too strong and strange to ignore. Most people can report similar experiences, but do not delve into the possible reasons for them. Most of us have had the experience of feeling that people or places are familiar, even though we cannot possibly have met or seen them before in this life.

Other possible explanations

With children, there may be cases of over-active imaginations, or the ideas being accidentally planted in a child's head. It may even be, more controversially, something called genetic memory. This concept theorizes that, if a parent or anyone in their genetic line has been to a place, the experience may have been registered in the genes that have been passed on. Along similar lines, there is controversial scientific theory being developed at the moment, which is exploring the fact that the experiences of your parents and grandparents can modify the DNA they pass on to their offspring. This does not sound likely to me, but who knows what science will reveal in the future.

For adults, the suspicion is also that books or films may have been read or watched, showing the place, or people in question. The information absorbed may have been temporarily forgotten, but the content mistakenly stored as experience, rather than fiction. It may also be a case of false memory syndrome. However there is simply too much evidence out there, albeit anecdotal, to dismiss as a complete nonsense the concept that we have lived before and experienced different lives.

If it does happen, then why can't we all remember when we have lived before? I learnt later that the theory is that memories of past lives are said to be wiped before every new reincarnation. You are literally re-born with no memories of who you might have been before. Sometimes, though, the memories or realizations begin to seep though into our current consciousness, which is what happened to me.

If it is in us all, how can we find out about what lives we have led? How can we prove it to ourselves? For adults there seems to be two ways of accessing information from past lives. These are memories surfacing out of the blue or people deliberately seeking out and trying to retrieve past life memories.

Returning memories

In the first case, the memories creep back on their own, or suddenly and unexpectedly re-surface. This happens in dreams, unexpected skills or fears or déja vu. How often have we been to a place and recognized it although we have never been there? How often do we 'recognize' people whom we could not possibly have met?

There are always other explanations for such things, of course, but not all can be explained away. For me, my memory of drowning trapped under a boat came about, out of the blue, in the course of a Reiki healing session. I suddenly, and unexpectedly, felt the weight of the beam on my chest and realized that I was trapped and would be drowned. There was a sense of frustration of things left uncompleted in that life. It also explained the feeling of dread that I always experienced when I was on board a sailing boat. I love the water and had no fear of falling in, but I feared bumping in to other boats and capsizing. I also 'know' that I have tried to write this book before and have not completed it. Somewhere in the North of England there is a note book that I have left in the library in a big house. One day I will go and try and find the house and it!

Deliberate unlocking

In the second case, people who feel subconsciously that they have lived before go and seek out a specialist practitioner to help them unlock these unremembered lives. This is sometimes done because they have mental or physical problems in this one. It also sometimes happens that people seek some other form of mental therapy for problems, and are shocked when past life 'stuff' comes out unexpectedly.

My husband was, in his words, 'mesmerized', by a friend of his then current girlfriend many years ago. He was working with her, as part of his business to promote a meditation music CD. This regression was offered as a treat and he felt that it would have been churlish to refuse. He was very sceptical beforehand but, to his surprise, several lives were revealed to him. This included a Paleolithic one, (not much going on then apparently) and most significantly for him, an American Civil War one. He remembers being in the stables and seeing one of his now current friends in this life. He also saw a figure he called the Angel of Death. Toby then felt that he took a cannon ball in the stomach and was killed. Strangely, he was born with stomach problems in this life. Is this linked? Very possibly.

Personal regression

I myself tried regression, just to see, whilst writing this chapter. It is a strange experience and two lives were revealed. These were a mercenary life in Roman-occupied Britain and a life as an army general in a battle, probably Agincourt. Did I believe in it? Well these lives, and the opinions expressed, could explain certain attitudes and relationships with people now. Insights and attitudes that I had from an early age, which were certainly not a product of my upbringing or education or even obvious genetics, were possibly explained. Could it have been my imagination or my mind playing tricks? Absolutely, this may be a possibility. I have no way of checking up, but it was certainly interesting.

Further evidence

In my researches I came across two interesting concepts which give some credence to reincarnation making sense in an alternative big picture of the universe. These were the concept of Karma and something called the Akashic records.

Karma

This is another talked-about phenomenon, touched on in the previous chapter by Simon, which is implicit in some other cultures, especially Buddhist. Karma involves the theory of moral causation. The theory states that past actions in previous lives can affect us now. Each person is rewarded or punished in this life, according to their previous deeds in others. Karma does only make real sense if we do live multiple lives.

We often, in our culture, jokingly talk about an action having good Karma or bad Karma. Certainly, from my experience, I have observed that people who behave badly do almost always suffer the consequences long term, even if short term they do seem to get away with it. Vice versa also seems to apply. It is even more interesting if we are punished or rewarded not in this life but the next.

Multiple lives, multiple types of life, rich or poor, lucky or un-lucky, male or female; if we believe in reincarnation then Karma does make sense. If it is a method of learning across many lifetimes; it may indicate why some people seem to have particularly bad or good lives without seeming particularly to deserve them.

The Akashic records

Similarly, there is discussion in some esoteric and spiritual circles of the existence of something called the Akashic records. This concept is also considered to be Buddhist in its origins. The Akashic records are supposed to be a 'database' containing all knowledge of human existence and the history of the cosmos, past and present. These records are to be found in the non-physical plane of existence. They can be likened either to a super-computer, or to the mind of God. Some people talk of them as being a type of etheric consciousness. Evolved beings can allegedly access them through astral projection. Does this mean that everything, in all lives, has been pre-planned? If so, by whom and for what purpose? The concept is impossible to prove or disprove, but certainly indicates a bigger and stranger ulti-mate reality than that which we usually consider, if it were to be true.

Could multiple lives, Karma and the Akashic records be possible? The answer is, of course, that it depends on the actual big picture of the universe. This we cannot yet know. All we can see are the reflections of this strange alternative reality half-remembered by some of us. If they are the truth, then it does indicate a vaster, more complex universe than our conventional teachings would allow. If we reject the conventional religious dogma, then what is the point of our existing at all? Why on earth would we be living multiple times? There must be a purpose and a plan behind it.

Aspects of reality

- A part of us, our essence or soul, leaves our bodies after physical death.

- We seem to go to another, unknown, dimension after death.

- There is growing evidence that we then re-incarnate and live multiple lives.

- It is not known why we should do this, or who causes it to happen.

- The memories are still somewhere in our consciousness and can be accessed accidentally or deliberately.

- The purpose of these multiple lives seems to be to experience and to learn lessons.

- The concept of Karma seems to balance actions and consequences, both within and between these lives.

- If the Akashic records do exist then that could indicate a more planned and stranger reality than we can yet imagine.

It may be concluded that many people, more than the scientific community and some religious institutions would care to accept, believe that we live many lifetimes; though we cannot know what the reality of the strange big picture of the universe, as hinted at above, could possibly be. It does in the end depend on our true origins. It depends on the real story of how and why mankind came into being.

To try and shed a glimmer of light on our true origins and purpose, I went back to a different and more basic beginning. Where can we prove we came from? Where did our planet earth come from? What is the true story of our creation? Could there actually be hard clues to our ultimate reality there? What do we actually know, for sure, about the physical origins of earth and humanity itself?

CHAPTER EIGHT

The material big picture

Where do we think we are? What is our place in the universe? Where did we, and our universe, come from? These are the next important questions to be looked at in this chapter. We are taught that mankind inhabits a smallish planet that we call earth. This earth seems to be part of a solar system of other planets orbiting around a medium-sized star we call our sun. This sun is part of a galaxy consisting of billions and billions of other stars. Our galaxy is known as the milky way. In the total observable universe there are billions and billions of galaxies such as ours. Scientists have not yet detected an end to them, even with stronger and stronger telescopes. We have not yet found the limits to the total universe.

The big questions

What do we actually know about this earth and where it originated? How did it come into being? All we have for hard evidence are the facts as proposed by the scientists who study these things, and of course the religious theories. Where could the truth lie? The proper answer is, of course, no one actually knows for sure. Whatever discoveries and statements are made by scientists and explorers, they are limited by the tools available, plus the state of knowledge and imagination at the time they are living in. Although the finest minds propose theories which are considered sound by current understanding, we can never be wholly sure that our information is accurate. Things change, new discoveries come and challenge what was assumed before about our origins and physical existence. The most fundamental assumptions may be challenged by new discoveries in science; sometimes these even seem to contradict what has been held as fact before. After all, the finest minds once thought that the earth was flat. Although that sounds ridiculous to us, some of the theories we hold today may be considered just as silly in the future.

All we can do is to try and make sense of what is actually said about the physical world around us, that is our own planet and habitat, and put it in some sort of context. The next step in our search is to look at, and evaluate, what science and religion say about how we got here in first place. This may give us the clues we are looking for concerning the nature of our reality. How can we go about answering these fundamental questions? To make sense of any of it, we can only start with the physical evidence available.

What do we actually know for sure? We appear to be living in a complex environment on this planet earth. Earth does seem to be set up to sustain life. Our physical bodies are nurtured and sustained by eating the plants and animals that we find inhabiting this planet with us. I looked first at what science and religion had to say about our probable origins.

The religious view

At school and in church I was taught that our God made us and all around us. According to the book of Genesis in our Bible, he said "Let there be light". Then the creation process began. At this point, we are told, he brought the physical earth as we know it into being. Then, out of chaos, waters were parted, dry land came into existence. After six days, earth was fully furnished with plants and other animals to be able to sustain life. We were then created, planted on earth and given a soul and dominion over all the animals. There is no direct proof offered for this theory. It is considered only a matter of faith. Other religions have similar faith-based creation theories.

The view of science

Growing up, we were taught the then scientific mainstream theory of the origins of the universe in science lessons at school. This, of course, was a totally different picture. The universe is said to have come into being with a so-called Big Bang. This Big Bang theory refers to the moment when the energy from which the universe is made burst out instantaneously from a single point, into what was previously empty space. Eventually, the theory goes, as energy cooled into gas then dust, our earth was formed alongside the other planets around our star, and eventually became fit for humanity to survive and thrive on. It is well worth mentioning here though that some experimental physicists now do not believe that the Big Bang happened, or if it did, not in the way mainstream science believes. This is still generally the scientific view of creation, though.

These creation alternatives, science and faith based, were all that was then on offer. There was no thought to reconcile both these ideas. Certainly no one thought it was necessary then. I remember even at a young age, rather simplistically, thinking that there need not be a conflict as God could have triggered the Big Bang which caused our eventual creation on earth. This idea, I understand, is now accepted in most religious circles.

Which of these theories is there most evidence for? Could science or faith, or something completely different be the right answer? To try and understand the truth of the matter, we will have to go back as far as we can, to the beginnings of our known time. The pivotal question is then, did someone make and design the universe in which we live, or did it spontaneously and randomly make itself?

What do we know for sure?
Even in my lifetime there have been several different scientific ideas concerning how our universe began, and how matter solidified into stars and planets. Stronger and stronger telescopes and probes are always trying to expand our knowledge of what is out there. Physicists and astronomers are all working to push back the boundaries of our knowledge. The known universe seems to consist of groups of stars formed into galaxies with seemingly empty space between. There are literally millions of galaxies, some round, some spiral. We cannot see

the end of them yet. Even the strongest telescope has not found the limit to the universe. In these galaxies there are also suns with planets circling which may or may not support life. Our own galaxy and solar system, sun and planets, are just a small part of a gigantic whole.

When did the universe come into being?

What we think we know is, that the creative bang, if it did happen that way, took place thirteen to fourteen billion years ago. Pure energy allegedly burst forth from a point. After a brief period of expansion the energy travelled outwards, cooling, filling and forming the universe. Apparently, all things today are still rushing away from each other. All the stars and galaxies are still moving apart. This is happening at a uniform speed that can be measured. It shows that the universe is still expanding. Traces of the radiant energy left behind can apparently still be detected. By working things backwards, scientists have calculated when they think that the bang occurred. There is, however, a question about where in the universe this event actually happened. Although I certainly always visualized a bang in a central point, there is also a theory that it happened everywhere in the universe at the same time.

Singularities

This exploding bang point is a something that is almost outside of our current scientific understanding. Energy/matter in it must have been compressed to a point at extreme pressure and density. This point is referred to as a singularity. Most interestingly, there are currently other strange singularities existing in the universe now. Mere points in space, they are hot and dense beyond our imagining. Small singularities are suspected to exist at the core of something called black holes. Black holes are areas of intense gravitational pressure. They are black because the forces of gravity in them are so strong that not even light can escape from them. They pull surrounding matter in to them, even sometimes consuming stars. The intense gravitational forces inside them make the matter so dense that it is squished into what is called infinite density. (A strange concept which defies proper explanation). Even more strangely, it is held that at the point of a singularity, space, time and indeed physics as we know them no longer exist. It is suspected that there is a large black hole/singularity at the centre of every separate galaxy. It is worth noting that it is concerning the singularities and black holes, that the known scientific models come under strain. Einstein predicted the existence of black holes in his general theory of relativity, which explains the physics of the very large in the universe. Quantum mechanics, the science of the very small, explains the sub-atomic structures. The problem lies with the fact that, where singularities and black holes are concerned, these models seem incompatible. Nevertheless, these black holes do seem to exist. Some people even think they may have detected one.

The standard model of creation

How has science worked all this out? Cosmological science has a 'standard model', with which all scientists working in the field agree. Presuming that the Big Bang actually happened, how was the outward rushing pure energy supposed to take the solid forms that we see today? According to the standard model, science maintains that in the process of expansion, the energy cooled into dust and gas (mostly hydrogen), about five billion years ago. How did this become suns and planets? The theory is that the rushing energy became a sort of atomic fog. The emerging atoms cooled into gas and dust. Gas and dust gave birth to stars/suns, in a process which I will describe below. Suns formed into galaxies. Some suns acquired planets. Planets sometimes evolve, in Earth's case eventually developing a biosphere, life and us as inhabitants. That is the current theoretical scientific theory of why and how we are here.

The process of star formation

The process seems to be as follows: the theory is that the stars were formed by the dense parts of these dust clouds collapsing in on each other owing to the force of gravity. Gravity causes all matter to be attracted to each other, and is a vital part of the behavior of the whole universe. It is the force that holds us on the earth and stops us spinning off into space as the planet rotates. It is one of the key forces holding the universe together. The larger particles of these clouds would have been attracted to each other by this force, and a process of something called gravitational collapse would have begun. This is a tricky concept, but as I understand it, self-perpetuating. Seemingly, as the particles become bigger they have more gravitational pull and attract other particles even more strongly. Gravitational collapse means that the cloud of dust and gas would have got denser and denser, and pulled more of any other dust nearby into it.

The then emerging, heavier clouds would have clumped together and pulled even more surrounding material into them. The heavier particles would have collapsed into the centre and attracted more and more of the outer ones. The heavier the centre, the more and more debris would be pulled in, and on and on. As these compression and gravitational stresses were generated, the cloud form would have thickened even further and gravitational stress would have also caused it to rotate. The rotation would eventually result in a central core of denser material with a flatter dust disk around it. Friction and the gravitational forces would have also caused the emerging central core to heat up and up and a star would begin to form. Our own star would have followed this process. Further collapse and heating causes is it to get hotter and hotter at the core, and when the temperature reaches around twenty seven million degrees Fahrenheit a nuclear reaction begins. A sun/star is born.

Stars are natural nuclear reactors which convert the hydrogen atoms, which were there from the beginning of time, into helium plus energy. The energy is radiated out, giving us light and heat. Hydrogen has one proton (positive charge) at the core and one electron (negative and circling). Helium has two of each. As the sun heated still further and became a gigantic nuclear furnace, other elements began to be formed. Three helium atoms fuse to form carbon, two carbon atoms fuse to become magnesium and so on. These are the elements from which the planets, and ultimately our physical bodies, were formed. The suns themselves clumped into clusters that became galaxies. The universe we see today would have begun to be formed.

As astronomers look into the night sky they see stars and systems at different stages of life. They are also different sizes. Stars reach a point after billions of years in which all the fuel runs out. The generation of the power has stopped further gravitational collapse. When this stops the core collapses in on itself and the outer layer is blown millions of miles into space. This releases the matter that has been fused into elements. The larger stars burn more quickly and enable the heavier elements, including iron, to be produced. This is the stardust that becomes incorporated into new worlds. The iron in our systems comes from the dust of older stars. We are actually made of stardust.

Planet formation

If conditions are right there may be a remaining flattened dust disc which has not been used in star formation, around the sun. This may begin to amalgamate, by the same process of gravitational collapse, into planets or proto planets and other space debris such as asteroids. As the original disc surrounding the sun was flat, these would be on the same level or plane as each other, just as our planets are today. Science tells us that there were many proto worlds at that time, not just those we see today. Some became planets in their own right, some were captured by larger planets and became moons. Some were destroyed and absorbed and some became asteroids or other space debris.

The vital unanswered question

The above may be a relatively reasonable current scientific explanation as to where the universe, planets and stars came from, but it still leaves one completely unanswered question. That is, from where did the original Big Bang singularity, which started the process, come? For this, science has yet no proper explanation. There are some theories about multiple universes and matter coming from one dimension to another, but of course there is no scientific proof, even among the brilliant brains of mainstream physics.

Problems with the standard model

Another problem with the standard model of cosmology shows up when you look at what was supposed to happen moments after the Big Bang. Any explosion has hot and cold spots, and a vast variation in temperature. Yet our universe has been detected, by study of the ambient background microwave energy, to have experienced a relatively even temperature spread. There is a theory called inflation that tries to cover this by saying that the energy must have expanded and evened up first, before exploding outwards. This does enable the standard model to work, but not all scientists working within the field are happy with it.

To complicate matters, there are now further discoveries and a new generation of cosmologists are questioning the standard model. There is a dawning of an understanding that perhaps all that we thought we knew about the universe may in fact be wrong. There are things that have been observed and recorded in the universe that do not fit the standard model at all. For instance, the standard model held that it would be logical that, after the bang, the matter travelling away from the centre would eventually lose momentum and slow down. Gravity from the matter formed would help this process. Observation has shown that this is not happening; in fact all things are moving away from each other at increasing speed. Newly-noticed phenomena, called dark energy or matter, and dark flow may be responsible for this and other anomalies.

Dark energy and dark matter

For instance, it can be noticed when observing the galaxies, that some stars in them do not seem to do what is expected, according to current theories. In studying the spiral arm galaxies, astronomers noticed that the outer stars were travelling too fast. The gravitational pull of the bodies around us determines how we move in the sky. The astronomers and physicists felt that there should simply not be enough gravity available to allow these particular stars to travel at these apparent speeds, given the mass of the bodies involved. Dark matter may explain the discrepancy. What is this dark matter, then? Well, this is the mystery, they just don't know. It cannot be seen or detected. It does not emit light or reflect it. Scientists have worked out, to explain this excessive movement of the stars, there would have to be 5 kg of dark matter to every 1 kg ordinary matter. (How do they know such things?) But no one really understands what processes are involved here.

There is also a mysterious undetectable dark energy. Cosmologists have no idea what this actually is either, only that it exists. Deep space is not a vacuum, as was thought for many years, but seems to be filled with this strange stuff. The more the universe expands, the more this dark energy seems to move in to fill the gaps between everything. It is an explanation that helps to make sense of how things are actually behaving, but what could it be? There are many different theories, but no concrete proof it actually exists. Could it be anti-gravity? Or another force we have no idea about yet?

Super symmetry

This is another theory, which is gaining ground among physicists. Particle physics has its own standard model. This states that as well as our ordinary atoms there are twenty-four other known particles, which all have different functions in the cosmos. Super symmetry theory states that there must be another twenty-four with opposite spin, that we just cannot see or detect. This could be part of the dark matter, but nobody knows for sure.

Energy into mass

It is perhaps worth noting here that up until now there has been no proper understanding of why the basic energy that began the universe and became all of creation, ever achieved mass. After all, atoms are only pinches of vibrating energy; how could a whole universe be created, just from that? This has been a massive hole in our scientific understanding of creation. Scientists have been desperately trying to find what they call the 'god particle' the Higgs field or Boson. This is the theoretical particle, or field, that they think must give other particles mass. This has been searched for by scientists for over forty years and at the time of writing, the probable mechanism, which allows energy to become mass, has recently been identified. The scientists just do not know for certain. At research institutions, like the Large Hadron Collider near Geneva, Higgs Boson has been actively searched for and the researchers feel they may have identified it. Not all scientists were actually sure it existed, or exists in the form they have been looking for, however.

The case for the scientific theory of a purely randomly created universe from the energy of the Big Bang, thus does have some deep fundamental flaws. There are many puzzles that need to be solved before science can be 'proven' as the only possible logical answer to the mystery of creation and our very existence. We cannot totally dispose of a creator quite yet.

To clarify things further, all we can do is to look at the rest of the physical evidence available. We must look more closely at our own planet for clues. When did our earth actually come into existence? How did it get from molten rock to an inhabited planet? How did it gain a biosphere? How old actually is it? Could it have been created in one go, as per the religious stories?

Planet evolution

If you recall, from the dust disk around our new sun, earth was one of the planets formed by the same forces of gravitational collapse as the sun had gone through. It became a material but molten mass. This gradually cooled down and solidified over billions of years. Earth went though many stages before it became the planet that we live on today. The structure of the earth now consists of a dense core, a mantle of molten rock and a crust on which we live, which moves over the mantle.

Earth began as a hostile environment for any life. How does science explain how our planet became fit for human habitation? Of course it happened so long ago that no one can really know for sure. The current thinking involves a smaller sister planet called Thea colliding with earth 4.5 billion years ago. Allegedly, Thea crashed into earth causing our axis to tilt by 23 percent, thus giving us seasons.

She was destroyed and absorbed and matter was ejected, which eventually formed into the moon. The moon consists of the same material as our crust, which was apparently the big clue.

Paleontologists looking at the fossil record from four billion years ago found evidence that the world was spinning faster then. There seem to have been four hundred and ten days of twenty-two hours in a 'year'. Tracing back to impact time, it is calculated that the days were only six hours or so in length. The impact not only caused the earth to tilt, but made it spin like a top.

How did this help to change the earth into a planet which could support life? Allegedly, frozen comets crashed on the earth (according to one theory) thus giving us water and forming our seas. The theory seems to be that the moon was ten times closer than it is now, when earth was newer. This generated massive tides in the seas, which pulled and eroded minerals from the land and into the water. The rich minerals and nutrients in the rocks and soil created a primordial soup from which, scientists believe, life emerged. Though the one hundred miles an hour tides and the hurricane winds produced by the moon's proximity, would have made complex life evolving straight away unlikely.

Then the gravitational forces generated by the fast spinning earth pushed the moon slowly away into the position it is today. It is actually still moving. Reflectors placed on the surface by the American Apollo missions are sent a laser signal from a base in Texas to this day. This means that they can accurately measure the distance to the moon. The moon is moving away from us at 3.4 centimetres per year. The action of the tides hitting the land also slowed the earth down (tidal friction). One billion years later, the fossil record shows evidence of calmer seas, and therefore the existence of bacteria on the rocks. These were the beginnings of the plant life and animal life as we know it. It is thought that a particular type of emergent bacteria discovered photo-synthesis. This process uses light and breaks it down into chemical energy, with oxygen as a bi-product. Oxygen began to be produced in large quantities. This was poisonous for other emerging bacteria but gave us the atmosphere that we breathe today. This seemingly random sequence of events is supposed to have led to the emergence of life as we know it today. Plants, animals, insects, bacteria and man, living theoretically in balance and harmony.

How old actually is our Earth?

Current mainstream scientific thought tells us that it is about 4.6 billion years old. Could it actually have been created by God in six days? Days, of course, could be symbolic and mean time periods or eras. (But it could also mean a time period relating to twenty-four hours.) Genesis tells us that God merely gave instructions that the earth, sun and moon should be formed and they were. Scientists refer to the gradual process as described, happening over millions of years. Some New Creationist groups go much further and state that the creation of earth happened only between six and ten thousand years ago. There is apparently quite a debate. This new earth theory was apparently held to be true generally until the rise of analytical science in the 19th and 20th centuries. What is likely to be the truth in all this?

A technique called carbon dating is supposed to scientifically prove that the earth is much older than six to ten thousand years. The age of rocks can apparently be detected by something called Radiometric testing. This measures the rate of radioactive decay of isotopes of the chemical elements in the rocks. Some radioactive isotopes decay rapidly, but others extremely slowly and these can be used as a means of telling the age of rocks. For example, some granites in certain places have been dated as being several million years old. For organic matter, carbon dating measures the rate of radioactive isotope carbon 14. It has what is called a half life of 5,730 years (half the radioactivity present in the living plant vanishes in that time scale). So if a sample of wood only had half the expected carbon 14 it would be about 5,730 years old. This can be used for dating up to 50,000 years. For example, samples from the pyramids in Egypt have been dated and their age has been found to agree with the date of historical record. Therefore, use of these techniques seems to prove that the earth is old, not new. They prove that the earth could not be just a few thousand years old.

Of course, those who think it is newer would argue that this is supposing that these decays have always happened at the same rate. This is a fair point.

It must be said, though, that proving that the earth is old, not new, does not necessarily disprove Genesis. Science has postulated a logical chain of events as above, with the knowledge that we have today. Advances in science could reveal the flaws in our understanding of the creation process, or prove that it just could not have happened the way we have been taught. There may, however, be a breakthrough in scientific understanding that will prove that we got it right. There is actually also no way of disproving that the earth and universe did not just appear in their current or primitive form, as per the Bible.

Evidence for deliberate design

There is actually a bit of a strange clue, though, which may suggest a deliberate design (thus designer). There is a concept called the Cosmological Constant. This states that the laws of physics, which came into being at the time of, or just after, the Big Bang, are carefully balanced to allow the universe to hold form. Can this really be just a coincidence? If gravity, for example, had been stronger then the universe may have been too dense for life. If it had been weaker, then the stars and planets could not have formed or hold form. Other theories try to get round this problem by suggesting that or multiple universes may have come into being at the same time. Every one would have a different value for forces such as gravity. Only those which had the right mix (including ours) survived. This idea though, I think, may make the concept of deliberate creation by a designer more likely. It may also just reveal a stranger scientific big picture than we have yet imagined.

Other creation stories

We have discussed the science versus creator cosmological theories, but other cultures than ours also have creation myths. Whilst the scientific theories seem accepted on a worldwide basis, there is variation in other religious theories on the origins of life. In practice however, many other creation myths in other cultures have similar theories to our Biblical stories. The following are just a few that I have come across in my research. This is not a definitive list, but just a sample of what I found out there.

- The aboriginals of Australia have a legendary mother goddess that woke up the spirits of the plants and animals, then man, and placed them on the earth. She then went into the sky and became the sun.

- The Japanese have the tradition of a muddy watery earth, that acquired a germ of life which then grew green shoots and became gods that created vegetation. The gods then married and had children which populated the earth.

- Some cultures have myths of people living below the earth. They then emerge by some mechanism to populate an earth which was already furnished with plants and animals.

What these variations on creation stories have in common is that they believe that the world was already formed by a creator of some sort, before man arrived.

Kabbalah

On a different scale, the Jewish Kabbalah has an interesting pre-Big Bang creation theory. As it was told to me, in simple terms, this is the sequence. It begins with Ain, unmanifest potential. Then becoming Ain Sof, limitless expansion. It then turns into Ain Sof Aur, limitless light. This then contracted and became the singularity that exploded and triggered creation. Is this likely? It is certainly unprovable, but just as reasonable an alternative as other scientific or religious ones offered.

Wicca

Similarly, Wicca states "Before time was, there was the One; The One was all, and all was The One. And the vast expanse known as the universe was The One all-wise-all-pervading, all powerful, eternally changing". Wicca then maintains that the energy was then moulded into twin forms. A god and goddess were created. They formed energy into gasses. Gasses become planets, suns and moons. The seeds of life were then planted. (*Wicca* by Scott Cunningham)

This has some of the same strands as Kabbalah, (The Ain which became the universe) Or even our Christian God (another supreme entity, all-knowing all-seeing) But note, the seeds of life are planted, they do not happen by accident. Ain and The One, are they gods or designers or universal consciousnesses? Certainly science has no proper explanation for pre-Big Bang. That energy must have come from somewhere.

Non-religious alternative creation theories

- Spiralling Torsion. This is a theory that sees energy travelling in a circular form, until it catches a line in space. It involves an antenna-like network, utilizing or connecting to points and arrangements. These lines are guidance systems that draw other connecting lines. These lines connect in space as sacred geometry. This then forms a multi-dimensional hologram and then collects the energy that enables matter to be gathered and become intelligent substance. (Thanks, Lauren)

- Similarly there is a body of thought that I have come across (as in *The Secret History of the World* by Jonathan Black for example) that believes creation came about by the focusing of a consciousness. The belief is that mind preceded matter. That matter was formed from thoughts. Thoughts became proto matter, then energy, then liquids then solids. Then life began in a simple web of one cell vegetation which mutated and grew and eventually settled into the forms that exist today. This involved a soft body stage and hybrid forms which would not appear on the fossil record today. All of creation, then, is just a manifesting of our collective consciousness. Weird or possible? Before I began my journey I would have dismissed this out of hand. Later discoveries, however, have led me to understand that this may be more credible than would be apparent at first look.

This is not a complete or whole story. The alternative theories and comparisons made are just what my personal experience, education and discussions have led me to. There are no doubt more. All of them have elements of logic just as strong as our 'conventional' religious theories. It becomes, in the end, just a question of faith.

Has science proved God a myth?

Surprisingly this is not necessarily so. Science does not explain where the original singularity came from. Until science can explain how matter can spontaneously materialize out of nothing, then the existence of a God or an intelligent designer cannot be totally disproved. There are some theories concerning matter appearing from different dimensions, but that matter would have had to come into being somehow. The ultimate point is that God or some sort of designer could have triggered the whole thing. Science describes the probable mechanism of creation but cannot yet explain what happened before the Big Bang or why matter came into being in the first place. There are also of course the unexplained puzzles of dark matter and dark energy and the other mysteries we have touched on.

Aspects of reality

- Science has a reasonably logical standard model of creation from the Big Bang.

- Scientists think they can explain how the earth came into existence.

- Science cannot explain where the energy for the Big Bang originated.

- Science does not necessarily explain why pure energy becomes mass then solid matter.

- There are forces in the universe, such as dark flow and dark matter, which are hypothesized to exist, to explain discrepancies in the standard model, but they cannot actually be detected.

- Religious creation theories cannot be totally disproved.

- Factors such as the Cosmological Constant may indicate deliberate design of the universe by an outside agency of some sort.

We simply do not, and cannot, know the absolute truth about the origins of the universe. There are more questions than answers, even in the scientific model of reality. The origin of life, human life in particular, is the next clue to consider. We are probably our own best clues to understanding reality. The next question is then, what actually defines life, and how did it come to earth? This is one of the greatest, at the moment unanswerable, mysteries of all.

CHAPTER NINE

The mystery of life

One of the most puzzling of the aspects of reality I have looked at is the mystery of life itself. Why life, why human life? What is the point of it? What actually is it and when and how did it start? Whatever we know, or think we know, about the origins of the known universe and all that is within it, why life began is a great mystery. In this chapter I look at how science and religion explain the emergence and development of life on our planet. I also found some interesting alternatives to the conventional views.

The great puzzle is, why and how do a seemingly random bunch of chemical elements become the independent replicating entities of life on earth? I also considered how intelligent thinking life, a whole step up from the other animals, is said to have emerged. How could primitive life have taken the steps to becoming thinking human beings. How could this be possible? Could we even have had help? Matter and energy flows, rocks and stones, are one thing, but life, especially human life, is something special. The real understanding of what life is and why it seems able to exist, has great implications for our understanding of the nature of our reality.

The religious view

I, and most people I grew up with, were taught at church and school the conventional Christian religious explanation of how the earth originated. It was also explained how earth became furnished with vegetation and animals; God simply created all of it. We were told that when this was done, man was placed on earth and given life.

As the Bible says *"And the Lord God formed man of the dust of the ground, and breathed into his nostrils the breath of life; and man became a living soul"* (Hence 'dust to dust' when we die.) Life is then, in the religious view, nothing less than a gift from our creator God.

Other cultures, you may remember, have similar creation stories to ours. The actual order or method may change, but generally worlds, plants, animals and man are created, given life, and set to live lives on earth. The common theme is though, man, and all life was created and placed in position by a God, or a designer of some sort. The gift of life was not naturally generated, but put into mankind and all living things by an outside force. It came from outside physical creation. Some people believe that a soul/essence, that makes us human, arrives into our physical bodies, sometime in the gestational period. This happens either in the womb or at the moment of birth.

The view of science

Science says that we were made human after evolving from primitive life-form to man, over billions of years. Life was a natural product of random planetary evolution. Consciousness and the thinking minds that make us human are just bi-products of a developed complex brain.

The definition of life

To begin trying to throw some light on this conundrum, I asked myself some pivotal questions. For instance, how do you actually define life? How is it different from the rocks and stones and water around us? The definition is trickier than you might think. When asked, generally people would perhaps say things like, I know you are alive because I can talk to you. We know things are alive because they seemingly interact with the environment to sustain themselves in a way that rocks and stones do not, or do not need to.

For example:

- Life usually, but not always, independently moves in some way

- Life usually grows and reproduces itself by some means

- Although they sometimes co-operate, individual living things are closed and independent systems

- Living things take in nutrition from the environment to sustain themselves.

We know life when we see it, without necessarily being able to explain it. All we can say is that life, on this planet anyway, is generally organic, therefore cellular-based.

Cellular life

Cells are the minute building blocks of our organic life. They consist of roundish structures, with a nucleus in the centre. The nucleus is surrounded by fluid and the whole thing is enclosed in a membrane. All life on planet earth is made of either one cell or a collection of cells. The human body has between 20-30 trillion cells. We are multi-cellular creatures. Cells co-operate to carry out the biochemical reactions that allow life to continue and also reproduce. Each cell has in its structure a nucleus which contains the genetic information that it needs to do its job and to reproduce itself. We, and all life, are nothing but our cells in combination. There are many different types of cells in our bodies, doing many different things. They work in harmony to make us who we are as people, and allow us to thrive and function in the world as independent beings.

How cells are living structures

The structure of cells fulfills the basic scientific criteria that are used to distinguish life (animate) from non-life (inanimate). These are as follows:

- The ability to metabolize and release the energy stored in molecular bonds (which is what happens when we eat food and convert it to energy to power our bodies).

- The ability to form boundaries. (The individual cells that make all living things are enclosed structures).

- The ability to reproduce itself. This can be by just splitting or copy-ing cells or by some form of sexual reproduction. Rocks and stones cannot do this. They are considered inanimate.

We can say what is needed to be defined as organic life, as above. We can say what it is not. Does that however explain really what life is? Is life just a bunch of co-operating cells? Or is it actually more? Further questions then spring to mind. Are the three requirements for life as given above the only way to define life? Are there other forms of being that are sentient and alive, without us being aware that they are so? Is there life around us that our sense organs do not allow us to see? These are questions we cannot answer yet.

Once simple cells had formed, the next mystery was as follows: what drives the cells to organize themselves into animals, plants and human beings? If you believe that the first cells were formed almost accidentally, by natural processes, then why did it not stop there?

Reproducing and co-operating cells

I am told this is how things work. Within the nucleus of each cell in any organic creature or plant is a substance called DNA (Deoxyri-bonucleic acid) This is the substance that contains the genetic instructions used in the development and functioning of all known living organisms. Living things pass on their DNA in some form to be copied. A cell will split to reproduce, or DNA will fuse with other DNA in sexual reproduction. DNA is the code book of life. DNA can be considered the software in our organic bodies. In the same way that software programs a computer and makes it do things, the DNA tells the cells that make up our bodies do what they have to do.

Where does our DNA come from?

The make up of our individual DNA gives us all our individual characteristics. Every species of animal or type of vegetation has its own set of DNA within its cells. We, as individuals who get two sets of genes or DNA from our parents, have individual variations which make us look and sound slightly different from our fellow human beings. The wonder is that, receiving instructions from our DNA, each cell in the developing embryo knows what to do and what form to take. This is true for all growing things. Why do some cells become eyes? Why do some cells become flowers? It is all in the code within the cells produced by the DNA.

DNA is a double helix (a twisted spiral staircase looking arrangement). It consists simply of four chemicals which are always in pairs. Adenine with Thymine. Guaine with Cytosin. These chemical pair bonds are put in different combinations and sequences in long, long strings within our cell nucleus. Genes are just a name for functional units of DNA; they give us our inherited traits. The combination of all of the genes needed to make a functioning human being is called the human genome. Surprisingly, this was mapped for the first time a few years ago by Craig Venter, an American with his own foundation. The human genome consists of over three billion stepped pairs of these chemicals. We have somehow evolved from one cell to the complex creatures that we see all around us.

How did we get from single cell creatures to a 3 billion pair genome human being? What about all the life forms in between? The scientific view is that this happened by a process, first identified by Charles Darwin. The process is called evolution by natural selection.

Charles Darwin

Charles Darwin published his book *On the Origin of Species* in 1859. In this book he set out to describe what he saw as the natural evolutionary processes. Darwin describes a mechanism of evolution for plants and animals that now seems to be generally accepted. Modern evolutionists would say that becoming human and a thinking conscious being was just part of these developed evolutionary processes.

The Theory of Evolution

The theory states that life evolved in the following sequence:

- From the primitive but mineral-rich seas, the elements that make amino acids began to cling together in long chains.

- Single cell organisms began to emerge and mutate to form more and more developed forms of life.

- The primitive amino acids became the more complex DNA.

- Non-sexual reproduction began. Single cells reproduce by unraveling the DNA that exists in every cell as a copying mechanism. The DNA splits in half and finds new identical chemical partners. We are then left with two identical cells. That is how these simple organisms reproduce.

- Differentiation of life would have occurred. Mistakes are made in reproduction, some minor variations creep in. If these are more suited to the environment that they find themselves in, they are more likely to survive and copy themselves.

Over long periods of time the animals, plants or organisms change form and develop according to what gives them survival advantage in their environment. For instance, where there is a lot of nutritious nuts available, the birds that survive and thrive best are those that have the stronger beaks. They would then be more successful at breeding and therefore the stronger beak genes would be passed on at the expense of the weaker beak genes. If it was the only decent food source, then over time the beaks would become thicker and stronger (survival of the fittest). This is the way different species evolve. This sort of natural evolution can be the mechanism for explaining different variations within the main species. Sometimes the differences are so great that at some point the individuals break off and become the start of a separate species.

It is an interesting fact that all animals, complex or simple, have more or less the same complement of genes. We are only different because the genes are deployed in different ways. Why this should happen is not clear. We have 96% of the same genes as chimps, 75% as dogs and 33% as daffodils. (National Geographic Channel "*Was Darwin Wrong?*")

The Tree of life

Our planet's evolutionary pattern can be portrayed as a diagram that can be said to resemble a large leafless tree. This is what is known as the tree of life. It illustrates the progression from primitive life to the complex life forms, including us, that we see around us. From a common ancestor, all species of animal and vegetable life branched off and began to develop separately. The picture looks like a trunk with a few big branches growing out of it. From the big branches, representing main types, variations which became new species would emerge over the eons. These themselves may split or branch off. The diagram looks more and more like a tree with branches and twigs going up and up. Vertebrates, invertebrates, families and species, the differentiation went on and on.

Theoretically this is how the earth became covered in animals and plants. I have often thought how convenient it was. It is actually amazing, if you think about it, that primitive organisms randomly evolved giving us both animals, and the vegetation to enable them to survive. (Almost as if it had been designed that way!) Why did some microbes evolve into plants? Why did some become animals? The more you think about it the stranger it becomes.

Anyway, notwithstanding the many natural catastrophes, life on earth as we know it came into being. Many species (I have heard a figure of 99%) were lost on the way, as climate changed and conditions varied. The whole species of dinosaurs seems to have been lost, probably as a result of catastrophic climate change, brought on by a meteor strike on earth. Man emerged at the top of this tree. Only a small twig on the tree; we are part of the animal kingdom, members of the ape family.

Are we still evolving?

It may be of interest to note that there is still discussion amongst some scientists as to whether man is still evolving. Have we stopped, are we in our final form or are we still changing? The thinking is that because of factors like clothing and technology and heating and lighting and shelter, we are protecting ourselves from the very environmental factors which may drive any natural selection change. For instance, the development of farming, which ensured a regular food supply, enabled us to keep alive many physically weaker individuals. They may breed rather than be naturally eliminated from the breeding stock of man by natural early death. This could be seen to be changing the quality of the species overall.

To look into possible evidence of this, there is now something called the Human Genome project. This involves mapping human DNA. Genomes are the record of all the genes everyone possesses. Every cell contains the copies of these genes. By swab or blood test they can be extracted and looked at. By tracing minor variations, bloodlines can be traced back. This has also for the first time enabled some scientists to look at the genetic make up of multiples of human beings. They can then see if there are any favourable genetic variations occurring to indicate that changing by natural selection is still happening in man. Surprisingly they found that there were indications that the process was still happening. The Broad Institute in America found that in the last two hundred years changes had occurred in the genes for temperature regulation, skin colouring, etc, which indicated that we were slightly changing, as we had changed our environment around us.

Other scientists looked at people living in extreme environments. The Sherpas in the Himalayas living at high altitude, with only 60% of normal oxygen, were living and thriving due to a stronger circulation system which enabled their bodies to use what oxygen there was more effectively. We are still very slowly evolving, according to Darwin's rules. Does this prove that he was right, however?

Other theories and questions

Well, our knowledge of the past is formed mainly by study of the fossil record. Fossils record the bones of lost animals. There may have been many soft bodied or otherwise differently constructed animals with no skeleton. This would mean that there would be no indication that they actually existed. Their omission may compromise what we think we know about evolution in the past. Also, if life was deliberately generated, by whomsoever, it may all have been pre-programmed to follow in the sequences as described. Not by natural selection but by a planned programme. The natural selection element may just account for the minor variations that allow plants and animals to thrive in their particular environment. Could just evolutionary forces create intelligent and thinking beings? Life's true nature, I suspect, is both a gift and a profound mystery.

Darwin's theories do seem terribly logical, and may be the explanation for the mechanism of the evolution of man, until several other awkward questions are asked. These include:

• What really triggered the development of life? How can just a bunch of chemicals randomly produce life which replicates itself?

• To make the simple, starter cells to begin life you need amino acids, sugars and lipids. These are quite complex substances themselves. Where did they come from? Why did matter organize itself into these particular forms?

• Did we actually evolve from apes? Or was there a separate stream of development? Did they ever find the missing link? Why are there no hybrid human/apes? Or hybrid anythings?

• Why did apes stop at ape level, and we go on to develop higher consciousness?

• Is our level of consciousness necessary in strict evolutionary terms?

• Why did some primitive cells evolve into the vegetation that enabled the animal species to survive? Why did they not just evolve into the same thing?

- Why did we develop speech and the apes not, although they have the theoretical capacity to do so?

The questions are endless. There are also apparently some missing links between species in the fossil record. Some of these questions will of course be scientifically answered in the future. It does seem to be, though, that Darwin's theories are not the whole story.

When did modern man begin?

A few years ago something called The Scientific Adam and Eve Genome project began. It involved studying the DNA of men and women, and tracing back ancestry through the generations to find the origins of man. Apparently, by looking at minor variations in genomes, bloodlines can be traced back. I do not understand how this is done (other than it involves massive computer time) but they have traced the original men/man to at least 60,000 years ago in Africa. It was from there, the theory goes, that the ancestors of modern man emerge. Gradually they migrated north, south east and west, and eventually populated the world. Skin colour and build would have gradually changed according to climate and circumstances and diet (as per Darwin's theory).

Creationism

The consensus seems to be then, man did not evolve everywhere at once, but emerged from one area in Africa. This can be seen by some as evidence for creationism. That is the theory that the world and all in it were created by a God. Could this place in Africa have been the Garden of Eden? As before mentioned, even the Vatican has acknowledged that the two theories of evolution and creation are not necessarily incompatible. Darwin was describing a process that could have been triggered by god, or indeed any intelligent designer.

Intelligent design

There is another set of theories concerning the origin of man. This concerns intelligent design by another sort of creator, or even a superior alien race. Perhaps man may just have been planted in his almost finished form in Africa. Perhaps even a species of ape may just have been intelligently enhanced by an outside agency at some point in their development, to become the value-added thinking creatures that we are today. Some people even believe that our ancestors could have been landed from an alien space craft as an experiment.

Could God or science have the answers? To make sense of this we really have to look at what other evidence is out there. The truth is that even if all the raw ingredients for life are available, it is currently not known why this random mix of things suddenly become the primitive replicating cells, which are the basis of all life on earth. This cannot be emphasized enough. Darwin may explain how, but does not explain why.

Where did life begin on Earth?

There is not even total consensus from the scientific community that life began spontaneously in the shallow seas of primitive earth. There are also theories that life may have started in the deep oceans, away from the atmosphere, but with high pressure and temperature. Some people think that life may have been seeded, deliberately or accidentally, on the earth.

A scientist, Stanley Millar, managed to recreate what was thought to be the historic composition of the earth's sea and climate. This was done in his laboratory in America. Surprisingly, by creating a spark to mimic the lightening strikes on earth, primitive amino acids began to form in the lab vessel. This does not give any clue however why these amino acids suddenly might organize themselves to become life.

A meteorite landing in Victoria, Australia in 1969 was found to have amino acids in its composition. Could meteors landing in the seas have triggered life? Could aliens or an intelligent designer have deliberately seeded the seas to start life off? Or did things happen completely differently?

Artificially created life

Biochemists today are trying to create artificial life forms in the laboratory. They stated recently that they had succeeded. Craig Venter's laboratory managed, after years of careful experimentation, to create a new genome by putting together fragments of DNA. They then injected the new genome into an existing bacteria cell. The genome took over the host cell and started replicating. This was hailed as creating new life, but in fact had to use an existing cell to achieve its purpose. This brings us no nearer to solving the mysteries of random matter organizing itself into replicating life at the beginning of time. The how and why are still dark mysteries.

Chance or design?

What is the likely truth? Personally I feel that the life we have is so structured and balanced and complex, that it simply could not have occurred by accident. I refer back to the watchmaker allegory. The world, and we, are too well-designed to be a random accident. Darwin describes a mechanism of evolution but cannot answer, why? The real puzzle is, what was the trigger that pushed inorganic rocks and water into the beginnings of organic life? Why did that life become so diverse? Also I feel that the understanding of human consciousness is the conundrum and key to "life, the universe and everything." Why, as successful primates, did we need, from an evolutionary perspective, to develop the level of awareness and consciousness that we have today? The questions can go on and on. Is there a case for the Old Testament God? Not necessarily, but there is a strong case for an intelligent designer of some sort.

Gaia

There is another interesting concept which has to be mentioned. This is the Gaia Hypothesis. This postulates that the earth itself is an ancient sentient being. As James Lovelock states in his books *Gaia*, and *The Revenge of Gaia*, the wonder of life on earth is that atmospheric and land and sea conditions are relativity stable to enable it to thrive.

Life on earth is powered by the sun, which fluctuates in intensity. It drives our weather systems and provides the energy for the chemical reactions that enable atoms to combine and reform, and to give us the diverse life forms and chemicals to allow them to survive. The puzzle is that the surface temperature on earth is on average constant enough to enable us to reliably grow food and support our civilizations. We are after all panicking about possible global warming of a few degrees, and the potentially catastrophic effect it will have on many of us. How is this relative stability achieved?

The textbooks will tell you that life on earth happened because we were just the right distance from the sun to enable conditions to be suitable. As Mr Lovelock states in *The Revenge of Gaia*, the sun's warmth was only right for life two million years ago. Before then it was too cold and afterwards it has gradually grown too hot. Solar warming is our real problem. It is the natural checks and balances he describes scientifically that have managed to keep the temperatures down and allowed us to thrive. What drives this?

For instance, we have just the proportion of oxygen in the atmosphere to allow us to breathe and survive. This is despite human activity which could alter the balance (burning fossil fuels etc). If the proportion of oxygen were any higher, fires would burn uncontrollably, any lower life would struggle. Also the sea has the right pH balance for life to thrive. The atmosphere has several layers and chemical adjustments are constantly being made at the higher levels to maintain the breathable and safe mix in the layer in which life exists. Can this be just a natural automatic process?

To complicate matters even further, there are those who would point out that Gaia is in probability a Deva, or nature spirit, as touched on in previous chapters. They would certainly point out that nature itself could not survive as it does without help from these spirits. If Gaia does exist, then the theory of life, however you define it, being just a random accident is totally disproved.

Strangely, it has to be asked, could a sentient planet have designed the life upon it itself? This may be part of a big picture that we do not even know exists.

An organized Earth

We have complicated bodies, but co-ordinate them through our control centre, our brain. When we walk, minute adjustments are being made constantly to enable us, strange two-legged creatures, to balance. Does the earth then have some control centre that does all these millions of large and small adjustments that enable life to survive on earth ? Is this control centre a brain? A sentient being? Or could it be just a natural computer program designed, by a designer of some sort, to enable life to survive on some planets? Or is the balance that enables us to live here, just a random series of happy accidents? Planet earth would survive quite happily without life. The effort that it is going to to maintain us, can be seen as complex, and unnecessary for its own survival. This may indicate that it has been designed to do just that.

The other alternatives

There are at least two other interesting alternatives to consider. Firstly, we could of course, as beings made at base of just vibrating energy, not be actually physically 'real'. We could actually be one gigantic computer simulation. It may be possible that we are a world and universe created out of someone's vivid imagination. If that is true then our understanding of the concept of physical life may be totally irrelevant.

Secondly, there is also a school of thought that thinks that we ourselves, operating from a different dimension, may be our own designers. Reality may have been brought into existence by the power of our own minds. This does assume a completely different view of reality than we have looked at up to now, though. It assumes a different interpretation of the reflections of reality that we can see.

To conclude

In conclusion, if conclusion is possible, we just do not know how a bunch of naturally occurring elements became the simple life forms, that eventually became us. We can describe the process of evolution once it had begun, but are not yet understanding the how and why of life's real origins. No one, not even the cleverest scientist, really knows. I believe that the strongest evidence in all this is for an intelligent designer or designers. The forces which created the universe, made earth habitable, and created life from a random medley of chemicals, are just too complex to be wholly accidental. If human intelligent life was designed and planted on the earth, and not a random accident, then what could the alternatives be? An intelligent designer of some sort; even the Old Testament God of our mythology, may be a candidate. Similarly, an aware, but non physically manifest entity, may also be a possibility. We may even be an alien planting, an experiment, a computer simulation, or figments of our own imagination. Until we understand the real truth about the nature of life we cannot really be sure.

Aspects of reality

- We simply do not know enough about the origins of, and reasons for, life on our planet earth to be really sure what reality its existence reflects.

- Creationists would say that life on earth, and we, were created and given life by God.

- Science would say that life evolved by chance, or was seeded by a meteor.

- Darwin's theory of evolution by natural selection may explain some variations in species, but may not be the whole story.

- There are many other interesting creation theories that are not mainstream, but may be more correct than is generally perceived.

- Scientists have not yet been able to create new life from scratch.

- Science simply does not know why a bunch of naturally occurring elements became primitive cellular life.

Without absolute scientific proof, the only reflection of reality that I feel comes through strongly, is that there does seem to be a strong element of deliberate design involved. Who and what the designer is, is another matter.

CHAPTER TEN

Aliens, and inter-dimensional beings

The next important question then is, are we alone in this universe of ours? If we are not, who could be here with us, and what could their existence mean for our understanding of the big picture of reality? The reality that we were taught at school and church was that God made us, and only us. We were a one-off, God's only creations. I now know that some religions, including the Mormons, do believe that God created many worlds, not just ours. That was definitely not the party line in my childhood, however.

Whatever the real truth about life on earth, most people assume that we are the only type of intelligent creatures to inhabit it, and indeed our entire solar system. In this chapter I look at the possibility that we share our reality with visitors from other worlds or other dimensions. There is plenty of evidence, old and new, that this may be happening.

Life on other planets

Astronomers are now finding other suns with planetary systems in the greater universe. There are over 100 found so far. Although they have not yet found an inhabited, or earth-like, planet yet, it may only be a matter of time. In our own solar system backyard, there are two planetary bodies that may possibly be capable of supporting some form of life. Titan, one of Saturn's moons, has an hazy atmosphere, although the surface is very acidic. Europa, one of Jupiter's moons, has a frozen surface. Cracks in the ice indicate some movement and there may be a sea under the ice. This could in theory support some form of life, as yet undetected.

There may also be conscious life out there that is not in a form we could see or recognize. After all, the energetic beings, angels and nature spirits that we talked about in previous chapters have not necessarily had physical bodies. Whatever their origins and purpose, they seem to be intelligent life forms of some sort. Life may be out there but not as we know it.

Contact

People through the ages have wondered about other planets and possible alien contact with us. Our government has always denied the possibility of any alien contact, whilst keeping a record of and investigating any reported sightings of possible spaceships or UFOs. I understand that they may have officially stopped denying these now. Many reports of alien encounters made by the general public seem to have been ignored or derided, however. There are many private individuals and organizations that do take the possibility of alien visitation and encounters very seriously.

Science fiction, which I devoured as a child was, and is, very keen on the concept of interplanetary alien beings visiting us, for better or worse. It was always assumed that by year 2000 we would be in space and probably communicating with alien races. The talk of 'little green men' was almost laughable and I think perhaps it was half expected that when we conquered space, and technology improved, then we may actually have contact with other beings from other planets. The assumptions were that, if they were there, they would be recognizable as intelligent life (give or take any odd skin colour) and would actually be able to communicate with us on some level.

This, as we all know now, did not actually happen. The space programs were scaled back after we landed on the moon. Improved telescopes just showed greater and greater amounts of empty space and far galaxies speeding away from us. The universe is unthinkably vast, however, and although there are now dedicated scientists looking for planets, only a relatively small fraction of stars have been studied. I do not think any found so far have been considered earth-like enough to maintain life as we know it. In any case the distances involved are such that it would take more than a man's lifetime to travel to or from them. Distances between heavenly bodies are measured in light years. A light year is the distance light travels in a year. Light travels at 100 billion kilometres per second. In a year it travels 9 trillion kilometres. At that rate it would take 100,000 years just to cross our galaxy. It would require very advanced technology to make more than cursory radio contact, if even that were possible.

Other forms of life

Human life, as we know it, requires oxygen to breathe, liquid water and a certain temperature range, not too hot or cold, to exist. This is alongside lots of others factors, such as the correct atmospheric pressures. Alien life may have developed using totally different parameters. Even on earth there are many primitive, usually microbial, life forms living and thriving in hostile environments, where life of any type used to be considered impossible. There are those living in acid or high salt lakes. There are those sea creatures living in total darkness around the deep ocean thermal vents. Microbes have even been found in deep caves, with no obvious food sources. They seem to dissolve the rocks they are existing on to get the nutrition and energy that they need to survive. Alien life may be in any form and living by any alien parameters. We may not even be able to detect it with our scientific instruments.

SETI

Especially in recent times, many scientists have been searching for extra terrestrial life. Science, particularly private science, seems not to have completely given up on the possibility of its existence, whatever the government line. Indeed there is an organization called SETI, once government- now privately-funded. For over 20 years it has been looking for signs of alien life.

SETI stands for Search for Extraterrestrial Intelligence. The searching is done by scanning the heavens for radio signals, with massive radio telescopes. A vast new one with expanded capacity is now being built and brought on line in America. Others are being built world-wide. SETI are looking for any abnormal signals that may be 'man-made'. These have to be distinguished from the background hiss of natural radio waves emanating from the stars in our galaxy. Radio signals coming from space in a coherent form may indicate an advanced, or at least an intelligent, life form, that has a capability of radio transmission. Such radio waves would indicate that we are not alone. Whether it would be life in a form that we could recognize, or vice versa is another matter.

On 15th August 1977, in Ohio State University there was one such signal for 70 seconds. They call it the wow signal, but it has never been repeated. Does this mean that it was just an aberration? Not necessarily; with current technology we are only monitoring suns up to 200 light years away. This is only a minute fraction of the known stars in the Universe that may have an inhabitable planet circling them and therefore the possibility of intelligent life.

Other searches

There are also other scientists looking for light signals. An intelligent race may broadcast laser signals which can be distinguished from other natural light sources in the universe. They are similarly unsuccessful as yet. They are also hampered by limitations of their equipment and the range involved.

Evidence of visitations

Even though the distances involved would seem to render it impossible, strange beings that arrive in peculiar vessels have been reported through the ages. They have sometimes been welcomed and sometimes feared. They seem to have been, certainly in the development of what was to become modern western civilization, often regarded as figments of the imagination or myths, by the powers that be.

In recent times there does seem to be an official ambivalence concerning such phenomena. For years they were recorded and sometimes investigated. Almost always they are explained as natural phenomena, military aircraft or prototypes or dismissed as hoaxes or mistakes.

Generally though, evidence has been there but only anecdotally. There are those who claim to have seen strange craft doing strange things, which should be impossible if they were using today's technology. There are also those who claim to have seen, communicated with and even been abducted by various races of aliens. The truth of the matter is very difficult to disentangle from all reportings and literature on the subject. Even more so than with angels, there are some fantasists or cranks out there, who may claim to have seen fantastic things for the publicity. The sheer volume of reports by honest mainstream impartial observers, however, mean that the phenomenon has to be taken seriously.

Ancient evidence

What other evidence is available? There is evidence from the ancients. Ancient writings and reports carved into stone on ancient buildings give us some written clues. Take Biblical times; many people feel that some passages of the Old Testament could be re-interpreted to indicate reportings of visitors from the stars.

- The prophet Ezekiel describes having seen what could very well have been a spaceship in 592 BC. He described a whirlwind coming out of the north, a great cloud and a fire unfolding on itself. He also described the non-human passengers who sparkled like burnished brass (space suits?). An account of this is to be found in the fourth book of Ezra. This is one of the documents suppressed, or left out, by the compilers of the Bible.

- Another prophet, Enoch, talks about travel to distant worlds in the sky. His book was edited out completely from the Bible, and his words were lost to western scholars. They were only rediscovered as the early Abyssinian church had attached the Book of Enoch into its canon. He is stated to have ascended into the Heavens at the end of his life in a "fiery chariot". It has also been pointed out that references to God or gods appearing are usually said to be accompanied by wind or fire or noise. This is something that a 'real' god would not have to do. The wind, fire, smoke and shaking ground often reported would happen if a space rocket landed though!

- Similarly, many of the inscriptions and wall carvings from ancient times show figures with rays coming out of their heads or what seem like space helmets on. There was a whole art gallery of figures looking like astronauts found by Henri Lhote in the Tassili Mountains in the Sahara.

- The Aztec and Inca stone ruins also contain many motifs which could be space men or machines. They could of course be purely decorative.

These ancient writings and carvings are obviously open to many interpretations. Classical Biblical scholars through the ages would also not necessarily agree with the alternative interpretations. It is to be remembered, however, that those looking at these texts in the past would do so in the light of the technical and cultural knowledge of the time. They would certainly have had no conception of visitors from other planets or spaceships.

It is impossible to be definitive as to what the ancients may or may not have seen and recorded. We must always remember that history, especially ancient history, comes down to us ready interpreted. We simply do not know what went on in ancient times. We may be very accurate in our assumptions, or we may be completely wrong.

The truth is that there may be evidence from the beginning of our records of alien visitation or interference in the affairs of man. Other civilizations before us understood that knowledge and information had been lost. It is only our scientific incarnation that discounts such things. The Bible is a record of history and of men's lives as well as a religious document. It gives us what could be seen as clues to something else that could be going on other than that which the mainstream establishment hold as fact. The truth is that we simply don't know.

Ancient physical evidence

Many scientists and engineers are now saying that many of the ancient monuments in the middle east, including most famously Egypt and also the temples of South America, simply could not have been constructed without the use of high technology. Temple walls are level to amazing tolerances that could not have been achieved by hand. Huge blocks of stone have been moved and cut in ways that would be difficult even today, with our advanced machinery. This could either mean that our ancestors were more advanced than we give them credit for, or that they had help. Could the help have come from alien engineers? The problem is though, where are these tools or technologies? There is now no trace.

I must say though when I visited Luxor Museum many years ago, personally I could not believe that some of the artifacts were made by hand. It seemed inconceivable that they had not been machine tooled.

Other strange physical evidence includes the famous Nasca lines in Peru. This is a vast level tract of ground, with track lines stretching many kilometres. There are also several massive designs of animals of the time, which can only be seen in complete form from the air. Some think that they were runways for space travellers and signs or messages to the 'gods' or astronauts.

Alien technology?

There is a school of thought existing among some ancient alien researchers today, that some technology now being developed may have been in existence when these monuments were being built; in particular the laser, and the sonic and anti-gravity technology which is being worked on today. The massive stones may, indeed some believe this is the only possible explanation, have been put into place using anti-gravity machines; what was thought of as magic may have been advanced technology.

Some of the weapons described in myths and legends involve spears from which fire sprang. Could they have been lasers? Were the walls of Jericho destroyed by sound waves? The American army and navy are using a sound weapon today in dealing with Somali pirates and in Afghanistan. These technologies may have been brought to help by these 'gods' from other worlds. Strangely enough, they may also have been remnants of older civilizations of our world. There is a theory, and some evidence, that civilization has been at our level before and been destroyed. We may never know the truth of these matters. All we can do is try and interpret remaining clues.

Alien intervention

This does bring us back to another interesting concept, though. That is, as touched on in a previous chapters, that it was alien intervention, not God or natural selection, that may have allowed us to have made the jump from primitive, naturally-evolved man, to the intelligent thinking beings we are today.

There is a theory that a superior alien race altered our DNA, which gives us our inherited characteristics, to enable this jump to happen. Could that be possible? We do a form of primitive genetic engineering ourselves these days. Who knows what may be possible in the future. This possibility does pose interesting questions about the true nature of the reality of our origins, though.

Some people believe that ancient Sumerian cuneiform tablets give detail of intervention from people from beyond Neptune who helped them start the Sumerian civilization. These people had allegedly visited eons before to alter primitive man. We were supposed to be a slave race to help them mine the minerals they needed to enable their own planetary survival. Is this possible? There is no way we could possibly know, but it is an interesting theory, backed up, allegedly, by evidence set in stone!

Modern clues

In modern times the pictures and clues become even more complex, It was in 1944 that non-aggressive 'foo fighters' were reported buzzing and flying in formation with allied planes in the second world war. These were balls of light. Were they UFOs or prototype enemy weapons? No one seems to know to this day. It is rumoured that the

Germans were attempting to produce a type of magnetic weapon. The confusion arises because surviving top German scientists were poached by the Allies at the end of the war. This was because they wanted them to work on their own weapon development. Secrecy, especially concerning what they were actually working on, became the norm.

In 1947 the first sightings of flying discs began to be reported in America. There were over fifteen hundred reports of daylight sightings that year. That, of course, was also the year of the famous Roswell incident. An alleged crashed flying saucer was dismissed as a crashed weather balloon. This was despite witnesses talking about unusual materials. The way the American Government handled this, and other incidents, was not straightforward. Whilst purporting to study the phenomena by starting the 'Blue Book', recording sightings and occurrences, they sought to play down or ridicule all that was happening. Explanations that were offered were often simplistic, for instance:

- In the famous Roswell Area 51 case, when there were reports of crashed spaceships and dead aliens, it was officially maintained that crashed weather balloons must have been mistaken for spaceships.

- Air force officers who reported seeing strange lights, were told that they had mistaken fire flies trapped on their windscreens.

- In 1966 sightings of a UFO landing in Michigan were dismissed as swamp gas.

- A close friend reported to me that someone they knew in the South African Air Force often saw strange things in the sky when flying that simply should not be there. He and his colleagues learnt to say nothing for fear of demotion, ridicule or even losing their jobs.

- There were also the strange cases of farmers reporting mysterious cattle mutilations at the time of UFO activity. No convincing explanation was ever given for these.

These are just a few examples that exist; there are many many more. Credible witnesses were time and time again ignored or discredited. People are, in the end, concerned about upsetting the status quo or standing out from the crowd. However, the sheer volume of recorded credible sightings by sensible people, especially those people who had no interest in the phenomena until they saw something, cannot wholly be ignored.

What could have been going on? As I understand it, Roswell was not far from Area 51, the secret USAF base. There is a strong suspicion that the US government were using the cloak of UFO sightings to cover up the testing of its own experimental aircraft. This was especially true in the Cold War. At the same time it was ridiculing the phenomena. Why? One explanation is quite simply that they were using alien technology and could not admit to it. In doing so they would lose their defence advantage. Were there also 'real' UFOs that were visiting? Was this just a gigantic double bluff? It is simply impossible to tell. Also, if national governments were to admit to the existence of visitors from other worlds it would change the status quo and would undermine too much self-interest. There are similar stories in the UK. Credible, sensible witnesses being ignored or hushed up. People also being afraid to report things for fear of ridicule. It may just be a covering up of our own government's experimental defence craft, or it may be something completely different.

It can also be asked why these things are not reported in the media if they are still happening? They were extensively recorded in the American media at one time. The topic seems to have been dropped or ridiculed. They are reported extensively on the Internet and in specialist publications. Mainstream press does seem to ignore such phenomena these days. You must remember however that the news that is reported to us is never the whole story about everything. Topics are picked up and dropped by our press and media according to hyped news values and fashion. Still considered cranky or silly or dangerous by the powers that be, the topic is, with occasional exceptions, ignored. It is worth bearing in mind that the media empires are controlled by a very few powerful mainstream moguls. The answer may be even more sinister than that, though. The topic may have been officially suppressed. It may also have just been discarded because it was thought to be too silly.

Alien interaction

There are also the reports of actual interactions with aliens. Strange figures have been seen, telepathic communication is alleged to have been received. Huge numbers of people report that aliens come for them at night and take them to spaceships to monitor and examine them. Several types of alien have been identified, including the infamous 'greys'. Many such stories have been retrieved under hypnosis. People have been aware that something strange has been going on but not sure what until their memories have been unblocked. Again there is no scientific proof, but a lot of anecdotal evidence.

Is this likely? Who knows? but something very strange is happening to a great many people. If there are alien races out there with superior technology, then it would be reasonable that they may be observing us, in the way that we would monitor and observe primitive tribes. Only very advanced races could cover the distance involved in less than our life time. They could, of course, be very long-lived races. It would also be reasonable to suppose that they would seek not to intrude overtly on our culture or way of life because of the effect overt meddling would have on us. If this is happening, we must hope that aggressive races that would see us ripe for colonizing, do not find us first!

What else could be happening?

There may be other explanations for the arrival of some of our alleged visitors, however. There may be explanations that indicate a totally different reality from that which we have been taught exists. You may remember that some reported sightings of craft and people describe them as coming from nowhere and disappearing from sight instantly. This may just be mega-fast technology or some instant transport system. It may however indicate something even more interesting. That is, the possibility of inter-dimensional travellers.

Inter-dimensional travellers

Our world seems to function in three dimensions. Everything has height, breadth and width. We, and all around us, are 3D. We see in three dimensions, and our brain can only process things in the three physical dimensions, and the fourth dimension of time. The theory is that there may be other dimensions around us that we are not aware of or just cannot see. Science is, after all, moving towards the possibility of a multi-dimensional universe. There may well be dimensions of space, and other universes around us, that our primitive sense organs and machines cannot detect. Could there be interaction from beings from these unseen dimensions? Is this a practical possibility?

I have come across a very interesting concept recently called Flat Land. (Michio Kaku - *Hyperspace*) This asks us to imagine a world of only two dimensions. People within it would be completely flat. They would have no awareness that there was another dimension, one of height. To imprison a flat-lander all that you would have to do is draw a line around him. He would not be able to jump or step over the line. A three dimensional being, however, could just reach down and pick him up. He would not see the hand coming, it would just appear from nowhere. He would not see the hand in three dimensions, he would just see a set of loosely connected rings. His eyes and brain could not properly process what was happening to him. We would be in the same position if we were contacted or visited by beings living in a world of different dimensions. They would appear to come from nowhere, and would not be in a form we could necessarily understand.

Personal evidence

As ever, when you openly ask people around you if they have had any experiences of aliens or UFOs you get interesting responses from people who have often not talked about their experiences before. For instance, someone I knew once described to me experiences she had been subject to. Several times a vast ball of orange light had flooded her house. It also came to her once whilst she was travelling in a car. She had an intense feeling of being watched. Was it an inter-dimensional probe? Was it just a strange natural phenomenon? It simply was too intense and unexpected to be just a trick of the light. Other friends of mine saw fast travelling balls of intense light when they were camping in Somerset. These are just two small examples. There are many more reported on the Internet and through other media. Many people who have had strange experiences which indicate something going on other than what they have been taught about the world, are just too afraid of ridicule or disbelief to mention it. When you ask outright, it is often as if floodgates are opened and people are desperate to share these things with you.

If asked if had ever seen an Alien myself, I would have to say no, as far as little green men are concerned! Just recently however, I was sitting in a pub car park and I saw a girl of about 20 walking towards me. The sun just caught her face at a certain angle and it caught my eye. She looked as if she had a ridge down her face running from brow to chin down through the nose. Full face she looked normal, although she was a very funny pasty white. She walked to join her friends and merged in with the crowd. Was she from another planet, and trying to pass as human? Was she just a victim of a birth defect or a terrible illness? Or was it just a trick of the light or my own imagination? Very hard to tell, I will never know for sure. All I know is that she did not look quite earthly.

I must also confess that I have met people in the very high tech industries, for instance, that do not somehow seem quite human. Though super-intelligent, they cannot easily interact with others, or read body language or understand emotion. It has been suggested to me they have been sent from a more advanced civilisation to help upgrade our technology. Could this be possible?

The difficult questions

Sceptics who do not believe in the possibility of UFOs at all may ask several hard questions:

1. Why do some of these witnesses give slightly different accounts of what they see?

2. Why since the advent of Star Trek and other visual space science fiction, are more and more people seemingly reporting more sightings?

3. If we have been visited by aliens, why has this not been acknowledged by government?

4. Why have they not been on TV or in mainstream media, or inter-
   viewed on the radio? What do they look like?

Firstly, there is an interesting possible explanation for points one and
two.

If you may remember, we perceive the world around us by way
of our sense organs. The information we receive from our senses is
then synthesized by our brain into coherent patterns. How we interpret
the world is very dependent on the quality of both those organs and
the capacity and skill of our brain. It will also interpret things in
relation to that which we already have experienced. Both our brain
and our sense organs are limited. There may be many things in the
world around us that our primitive organs are simply not perceiving
properly. On seeing something strange, our brain simply interprets it
to us the best it can. It does this having searched through our 'database' to compare it with something we can recognize. People do see
what they expect to see. This also explains how, in ordinary life,
people who give eyewitness accounts of the same event will report
something slightly different from each other. This would be particularly noticeable with something completely strange and new, like
sighting a UFO.

Also, why have people not always seen these strange ships or
alien visitors? Why do they seem to do so now? The answer is quite
simple. People have always seen strange things but did not always
have the words to describe them. Our brains now have the images
and words for what it thinks it can see. The advent of science fiction
in the media has helped to put these patterns into our subconscious
mind. The ancients described what they saw with words and concepts
that they knew. A spaceship may have been a winged chariot. We
now see the same thing and call it a spaceship, because that concept
is in our consciousness.

There is a lovely story which I have come across recently. I do not know if it is true or just a nice myth. Anyway it does illustrate the point of all that I am trying to say concerning this topic. Allegedly, when Columbus's ships were on the way to America they called at a primitive island. They dropped anchor off shore. The island natives did not know such things as very large ships existed, so they actually could not see them (no template in their brain). They could, however see the ripples or disturbances that the ships made. The Shaman (wise man) puzzled and meditated on the disturbances and gradually was able to see what caused them. He then showed the rest of the tribe who, because they trusted the Shaman, began to see the ships as well. We have to ask, what else is around us that we cannot see because we have no template in our minds for it?

Secondly, the answers to points three and four are more difficult to find. There are those people who would claim that they know exactly what an alien visitor looks like, and have posted pictures in specialist media and on the Internet. There are descriptions of aliens of all shapes and sizes. Some even look like giant insects. There are also people that claim they have been abducted or interfered with somehow by aliens. For instance, Whitley Strieber, in his book *Communion: Encounters with the Unknown*, describes such happenings over a period of years. On the cover of this book is a picture of a bald, greyish, oval-faced creature, with huge slanting eyes and a pointed chin. I think this race of aliens crop up quite a lot and are known as 'the greys'. This seems to have no official acknowledgement though. If encounters happen as frequently as suggested, one would think that mainstream media would have broadcast pictures of some aliens, at least.

Notwithstanding that, there are things that have happened to people that have no proper worldly explanation. There are those who believe that governments have already made contact with alien races and are covering it up for their own purposes (probably defence). All I will say is that, at this point in time it is very hard to disentangle the truth of the matter.

Alien danger

It is worth noting a word of caution though. Any alien race with the capacity to visit or communicate with us, must be even more advanced than we are. Even on our own planet, history shows us time and time again, that when a developed race meet an relatively less developed race it is always bad news for the latter. They are taken over or exploited in some way. Certainly, almost always interfered with, according to the conquerer's standards. This is particularly true when the former are warlike, greedy or just feel that their interests must come first. Do not forget, white settlers considered black Africans a sub-species and in some cases treated them like animals not so very long ago. Stronger alien races could think the same of us and just want to strip our mineral wealth and resources. To many developed races our world with its inequality, poverty and seemingly perceptual wars and squabbles would seem very primitive and backward. The famous cosmologist Stephen Hawking has voiced his unease at this matter.

It may be better just to keep our heads down and remain unnoticed in the cosmos. It may be too late, however. There are at least two probes that we have sent travelling across the universe that have information on them which identifies us, and where we have come from. In 1992 Pioneer 10 was sent out from earth on a voyage of exploration. It is now over 13 billion kilometres from earth and travelling towards a red star in the constellation of Taurus. There is a plaque on its side giving a map of where it has come from, and also a representation of us as humans and a representation of a hydrogen atom. Similarly, Voyager 1, now even further away, has a disc with representations of life on earth. We could be traceable!

Aspects of reality

- We are too far away from the nearest star or planetary system to make contact ourselves.

- There is evidence that we are not alone and have been visited throughout the ages by extra-terrestrial visitors.

- Some people feel that humanity has even been interfered with historically, either shown how to organize ourselves, or even that we have been upgraded into intelligence by interference in the human genome.

- Inter-dimensional travellers may be a possibility.

- There has been no official acknowledgement of the existence of, or contact with, any alien races.

- Aliens may be all around us, but invisible to us due to our limited sense organs or the filtering out by our subconscious mind.

- If there are superior races out there, we must hope they do not want to colonize us.

I myself have not positively seen a definite inter-dimensional being or an alien of any type. But all my life, I have felt or seen the ripples and known that they were there. I have known subconsciously that the world we are taught exists is nowhere near the whole story. Are we alone? Are there other dimensions and beings around us that we cannot see? Are we a product of Alien intervention? Has human civilization had help, and for what purpose? What does this mean for the big picture? The questions go on and on. How can we properly make sense of any of it?

The next important step in my quest for the search for the truth about reality involved going back again to basics. I looked at the science that underpins our notion of what the world and we actually are. This science, I found, was full of surprises.

CHAPTER ELEVEN

Strings, dimensions and other weird stuff

Any study of the nature of our reality cannot really be complete without looking at what scientific theories are on offer. In this chapter I look at what the cosmologists, physicists and other cutting edge thinkers have to say about the subject of the reality of our universe. Cosmology is the study of the nature of the universe as a whole. Currently, there are several main areas of scientific interest that may have fundamental implications for the true of the nature of reality that we find ourselves living in. I looked first at the grand scale cosmological theories. These include: string theory, multiple universe, multiverse theory and, strangest of all, the holographic model of the universe.

The role of physics

Mainstream physics, whilst not the whole story, also seems to offer some useful insights about the fundamental nature of things. We all know of the physical science of things that you can see. Most of us have heard of the laws governing fluids or thermodynamics, for instance. There are also branches of physics that interpret or govern things that we cannot see, but that people know are there. These physics deal with the fundamentals of our universe.

Physics is a way of mathematically quantifying and making sense of the physical universe around us. At advanced level it involves studying the composition of matter, both at atomic and sub-atomic levels. Cosmologically, it is also a tool that seeks to understand the bigger picture of the construction and interactions of our total universe. To make coherent sense of these actions and interactions, mathematical equations are designed, and models are constructed. There are equations which describe, amongst other things, how gravity works, how water flows and how energy is transformed from one state to another. You name it and there is an equation somewhere to describe it. This is the only way we can attempt to make sense of things in this world. This is particularly true for those things we cannot see in the vastness of the cosmos.

Field equations and forces

To look at the big picture, we have to ask how the complex forces that are detected by our scientific instruments could be quantified. One way of doing this is to construct so-called field equations for all known particles and forces in the universe. A field equation is made up of a collection of numbers, defined at every point in space, that completely describes a force at that point. Michio Kaku, *Hyperspace,* explains that "…three numbers at each point in space can describe the intensity and direction of the magnetic lines of force. Another three numbers everywhere in space can describe the electric field". As this definition implies, field equations are an attempt to describe the flow and intensity of any force and pin it down to a mathematical formula. To really understand the whole picture, we also need to know all the equations that these forces obey. This, in theory, can be done for all matter. It is an attempt to put into quantifiable number form, and understand, the mainly invisible forces and particles that are involved in the construction of our universe.

The unified theory of everything

The overriding aim of physics is to put into one great equation all the forces that govern our universe. The aim is for all of the theories concerning the known forces of the universe to be amalgamated into a compatible whole. This has not yet been possible. Until this is done, we cannot be sure that everything is properly understood. Until we know how everything really acts and interacts, then we cannot be wholly sure of the big picture.

For instance, there is Einstein's theory of relativity which sought to explain the physics of the large universe, and quantum mechanics which is the science of the small particles, atoms and so on. Coherently combining these, plus the theories of gravity, and strong and weak nuclear force, has been the great goal. This is referred to as the theory of everything, or the unified theory. It has not yet been possible to do this. The various equations concerned with these theories do not actually add up and make coherent sense as a whole. Something else must actually be going on in the universe as yet undetected, or we may just not properly understand the true big picture of reality. There are other areas of research, though, that may help to solve this problem.

The theory of multiple dimensions

The existence of possible multiple dimensions in our universe was first proposed by Georg Rieman in 1854. The very core of his work was the realization that the physical laws which seem to govern us become much simpler once we assume a higher dimensional space. That means a multi-dimensional universe. The quest to prove or disprove this theory has gone on ever since. Mathematical evidence is gathering, though, to show that these extra dimensions do exist. I am told that the equations used to try and attempt the unified theory are clumsy and very complicated. If other dimensions are assumed, and the equations are adjusted accordingly, they become simpler and more coherent.

The case for these extra, but unseen, dimensions becomes stronger and stronger. There could be people living parallel to us whom we just cannot see. There may be a physical higher dimension to which our departed consciousnesses travel on physical death. There may even be a heaven and hell. There may just be dimensions that our poor limited brains cannot actually understand. What some of us believe is a possibility, albeit with only personal and anecdotal evidence, may prove to have a scientific basis.

String theory

String theory states that everything, you and I and all around us, actually consists at its most basic level of tiny vibrating strings of pure energy. The protons and neutrons and electrons that we, and all the universe are made of are, as discussed before, are nothing but vibrating parcels of energy. Einstein's famous equation, $E=Mc^2$, simply means that energy and mass are, at base, the same thing. Mass (seemingly solid stuff) is nothing actually but vibrating energy.

This is a very complex theory but as I understand it, different basic particles vibrate at different frequencies. They are different notes on the cosmic string. The tricky bit then is the understanding that for the vibrational models to create sufficient of all the different particles there are in existence, there must be other dimensions in space for them to vibrate in, (other than our own known three plus time). The number of assumed extra dimensions are unknown, although theoretical mathematics suggests, depending on which mathematician is correct, approximately 13. Some theorists believe the total to be as low as 10, some think it may be as many as 26.

The next question is, where are these dimensions and what do they look like? The answer is that they must be here around us, although we cannot see them. They may be very small or very large, we do not yet know. They may be curled up or may be a just a proton away from us now. Our sense organs do not allow us to detect them. There is a clue apparently in gravity. Scientists think that gravity is simply not as strong as it should be. It may be leaking into these other dimensions.

Brane theory

This controversial theory takes things a step further. It states that all particles and forces are confined in our universe by a membrane. Only gravity seems to escape this. There may be other membranes containing other universes around us which we simply are not equipped to detect. Our membrane lives in a dimensional super-space.

String theory and brane theory are an attempt to bring together, and make sense of, the apparent anomalies between quantum theory (the science of the very small) and the theory of relativity (the science of the big picture). As ever, we simply do not know if it is the whole truth as to the actual reality of things, or just a partial understanding of a big picture that we have not yet grasped. Although there is of course, much controversy, the mathematics that may give credence to these theories are apparently beginning to stack up.

Multiple universes

This is another theory concerning the possible simultaneous existence of many universes. This theory refers to the existence, not just of other dimensions within our universe, but more than one actual created unseen universe along with ours. They could operate with different laws of physics. They could be totally separate from our reality. Or we may switch between them, unknowingly, as we progress though life.

Multiverses

This is a similar but more complex theory first proposed by a famous quantum physicist, Hugh Everett, in America in the late 1970s. This simply states that there are different realities, parallel universes, existing alongside ours. Our lives split into the different realities for every decision we make. If we decide between x and y, there will be a reality in which we do x and a reality in which we do y. These will split again on the next decision and there will be parallel lives generated in which we live alternative versions of our lives. Possible? Who knows, but it is certainly an interesting concept, even if fundamentally, at the moment, unprovable.

What puzzled me about this was, what would happen to our consciousness if this does happen? Does our consciousness split at this moment? Or actually are we just a sum total of all these consciousnesses, living all possible lives, in all possible universes at the same time? It is impossible to think about really. The debate is very current, and taken very seriously.

The universe as a mathematical construct

There are many variations on this topic, but generally the theory goes that nothing is random in the universe. It can be perceived as nothing more than a gigantic interlocking mathematical model. All of creation, and our earth in particular, are governed by mathematical rules. This can be referred to as the code.

All of creation, the way things grow, the way rocks are structured, even we ourselves, rely on set mathematical formulas and geometric forces. These include pi, which involves the measurement for circles, and the law of fractals, which explains how many diverse things grow, from trees to snowflakes. Many bigger systems which seem random, like the weather, are actually only chaotic. The patterns are there, but the variations are so many, and so complex, that in practice they are impossible to detect.

Some laws derive from the atomic structure of the matter that things are constructed from. The stars and planets operate according to measurable universal laws, such as gravity. These are so regular that it can be predicted what will happen in future, and also their paths can be tracked back in time.

The question is then, are these laws just inherent in the atomic structure of matter, or were they designed deliberately by a creator force to give the world we live in its current form?

The holographic universe

This is the most interesting scientific topic that I came across in my research. It poses the question: are we, and the universe around us, 'real' at all? After all, we do know that all we know and feel about the physical world is processed through our brains. We are our consciousness; it is the only means we have to know we exist as people. There is no proof that the physical world is there at all except within our minds. To recap, I looked almost at the beginning of my research at the nature of the physical structure of us, the universe and all around us. If you remember, we are constructed fundamentally from vibrating pinches of energy. As we are only energy beings there is a theory that we, and all around us, are nothing more than holograms.

The concept of all of creation being only hologramatic followed on logically from this realization that we are mostly empty space that appears solid. We think we are physically three dimensional beings in an overtly three dimensional world (not counting the fourth dimension of time). A hologram is a way of creating, with light, a three dimensional object which appears solid.

Many scientists have researched this fascinating topic. In the book *The Holographic Universe* by Michael Talbot, two particular front runners are cited. These are the University of London physicist David Bohm, a quantum physicist, and Karl Pribram, a neurophysiologist from Stanford University. Working independently, Bohm via quantum mechanics and Pribram studying the workings of the brain, both eventually came to the same conclusion concerning the holographic nature of the universe. Standard theories on the brain, and on the phenomena encountered in the universe which seemed to defy mainstream physics, seemed to them to make more sense if the holographic model was deployed.

What is a hologram?

A hologram looks real but it is not; it appears as a 3D image constructed from light. A hologram works when a pure light laser beam is split into two. The first beam is focused and then bounced off the object to be copied. The second half of the beam collides with the first. The resulting interference patten is recorded. It looks like a patten of concentric rings. It is this that can be reactivated with light to produce the 3D image. It is a quality of this holographic film that it can be cut into half or more and each fragment records the whole image.

How can this help with our understanding of the universe?

Well, Pribram's research on the localization of memory seemed to indicate that all memories were stored in every part of the brain. As every fragment of a holographic film actually stores the whole image, then the brain was exhibiting holographic tendencies. Further experiments also seemed to indicate that vision was not just computed through the visual cortex but was actually computed through the whole brain. Furthermore, he concluded that the branch-like formation of the firing neurons in our brain, with expanding and criss-crossing waves of electrical activity, may give the brain its holographic nature.

Not everyone agreed or agrees with these conclusions. There is still much scientific controversy. It may be, however, a realization that, as some mystics have always stated, there is a possibility that nothing is actually real in the way we understand it. It may well be that the world outside our brains is nothing but resonating wave forms which our brains transform into our version of reality. A very scary concept.

Then Bohm began to conclude that it was a basic mistake to view the universe as separate parts. There can be no real understanding of the phenomena for which scientists have sought to find a coherent answer, unless you look at the really big picture. There is implicit order in the universe. What we think of as random may not be random at all. It is only that we are looking on too small a scale. We are not understanding all the elements of the universe because we are simply not looking at the whole picture. This may include other dimensions. There may be a deeper reality that we do not see, which gives birth to the reality which we do see.

These conclusions may be controversial to say the least, but to me they have a ring of truth.

At the cutting edge of physics, which is supposed to give us the practical science behind a purely mechanical world, there is this sort of thinking. Indeed professor Hogan, in Fermilab in America, is conducting an experiment to detect a 'fuzziness' in the transmission of light which it is hoped will indicate that the holographic model is a possibility. It is worth noting that, if the holographic model of the universe is correct, then the concept and mystery of organic life, and how it began would be irrelevant.

Where are the originals?

Of course it does open up even more hard questions. If the universe is holographic, what is the original picture that it is a hologram of?

What does a holographic brain say about the nature of humanity? Are we just part of the hologram, or are we using the hologram to manifest as human beings? Is our consciousness, which seems to make us separate from our bodies still part of the hologram? Or are we just part of the whole and our separateness just an illusion?

Ancient ideas

These seem to be modern questions, but the truth is that for thousands of years there have always been individuals who have wondered and thought on the subject, even before science began to find possible answers. The ancient philosophers, brilliant thinkers of their era, were always speculating on the true nature of man and the world. This happened even before the nature and scale of the universe, as we know it, was understood.

For instance, Plato was born in 428BC. That is two and a half thousand years ago. His ideas are said to have influenced much of subsequent Western philosophy. Plato, surprisingly enough, denies the reality of the material world. He said that what we see is just an image or copy of what actually exists. We see shadows of the perfect world that exists (holograms?). He thought somewhere, at a different level of reality, were the originals of us. This was also where the 'forms' of everything lived. There were forms of all material objects. There were also 'forms' of abstract things, such as truth, justice and beauty. Gods lived in the realm of the forms. So reality has two levels – ours, and that of the realm of the forms. Is this any stranger than some of the possibilities arising from the other theories in this chapter?

Aspects of reality

- Physicists cannot yet tie together the many equations that describe the behaviour of the universal forces that make up our universe into a coherent whole.

- To make sense of things, a multi-dimensional universe is indicated.

- String theory, an attempt to combine the science of the very large with the science of the very small, sees matter as vibrating strings of energy.

- String theory predicts many dimensions unseen around us, to make sense of the mathematics.

- Brane theory and multiple universe theories predict that there may be other whole universes, which may have different laws of physics from ours, around us.

- The universe may be just a gigantic mathematical equation. Whether this occurs through chance or by design is not clear.

- Multiverse theory states that we live in an infinite sea of parallel universes. Also, every time we make a decision with different possible outcomes, we split off into two different alternative universes. This carries on indefinitely.

- The universe, and ourselves, may be nothing more than holograms.

- If this is so, where are the originals?

- If we are holograms, the mystery of organic life would become irrelevant.

These are all fascinating theories of some of the possible big pictures of cosmology. We cannot know which one, or ones, are true or likely. The really interesting mysteries, however, lie in the science of the very small. It is to quantum mechanics that I look next, in my search for insights into ultimate reality.

CHAPTER TWELVE

Uncertainties and the physics of the very small

There is a branch of physics which deals with the components of our universe which are very small. This is called quantum mechanics. Fundamentally, this is the study of the particles (quanta) which, in combination, are the building blocks of all matter. Underpinning all of creation is this science of the 'itsy bitsy'. Understanding how this works may hold the key to understanding what is actually happening on the very large cosmological scale. Quantum mechanics is a very weird world. The 'normal' rules of physics do not necessarily apply. In this chapter, I look at the strange unpredictable quantum behaviours. These include such topics as superpositions, non locality and entanglement and the ability of all particles to behave like waves. These all show that the building blocks of the universe are a lot more uncertain than most people realise.

The Newtonian universe

For hundreds of years, there was a widely held Newtonian view of the universe in scientific circles. Sir Isaac Newton saw the world and the laws of nature as a machine. His laws of motion are still valid today. The thinking was that there were fundamental rules by which the universe operated (like a machine). Things acted and interacted in predictable ways. Everything was, or would be, knowable and predictable if only we had enough knowledge of the input and the mechanism. The laws of physics were set in stone. The splitting of the atom and the dawning of quantum mechanics began to change all that.

CERN

An important source of research into these matters at the moment is the big CERN experiment on the Swiss/French border. The European Organization for Nuclear Research was established in 1954. It was set up to promote non-military fundamental research into atomic structure and to co-ordinate and sponsor international exchanges and co-ordination of information. At this present time it has developed the Large Hadron Collider near Geneva. This is a vast underground particle accelerator, constructed as a gigantic circle. Accelerators, as you might expect, accelerate particles. These are sent both ways around the circles at higher and higher speeds until they collide. The scientists cannot see or detect the particles normally, but in this collision they can record the fallout. They are studying the atomic nucleus and hope to unlock its secrets and really begin to understand the basic building blocks of the universe. As mentioned before, this is not really known yet.

Elemental particles

The search is continuing for the ultimate elemental particles that are the real building blocks of the universe. You may remember that for years the atom was considered to be just that. This thought persisted until scientists managed to split the atom. They then discovered the protons, neutrons and electrons from which the atoms themselves are made.

Similar experiments are on-going today in many places, including Fermilab in Chicago in America. Fermilab managed a few years ago to collide two protons in their particle accelerator Tevitron. To their surprise, the collision released literally hundreds of new particles of all kinds. This became known as the particle zoo. Further experiments found that all of these particles were a combination of six energy bundles called quarks. These were given names such as top, bottom, up, down, strange and charm. Ultimately, the standard model of elementary particles was found to consist of these six quarks, six leptons (some sort of cousin of electrons) and four particles concerned with force. These are the fundamental particles that make up all matter that seems to underpin our reality.

The mystery of light

Much of this research is very difficult for the non-scientist to penetrate or make sense of. This is particularly true when we consider the behaviour of the actual particles of matter. The nature of light, which we take for granted, is a great example. Light is the mechanism by which we see. A stream of photons, either streaming out from the sun as a by-product of its nuclear fusion, or streaming out from man-made sources of light, hits the rods and cones of the back of the retinas in our eyes and enables us to see. Our retinas absorb the light energy and use it for sight. Light is essential to our very existence. The problem is that these photons, along with all other particles, have the capability to act in total defiance of any normal, expected, Newtonian laws of physics.

Wave or particle?

The complicating factor is that light, as well as being a stream of individual photons, and obeying those rules, also sometimes acts as a wave. How can anything be both individual discrete particles and sometimes act as a wave? Waves can spread out over vast areas of space. How can energy particles be large, as well as small, at the same time? This realization was a catastrophe for conventional, Newtonian, physics. The true nature of the powerhouse of our life on earth, the light that enables us to function, is and was fundamentally a mystery. This paradox also applies to all known particles.

Quantum behaviour

Although the universe seems to hang together coherently, the behaviour of any given quantum particle is another matter. One of the first principles is that you cannot count on any particle to act in a predictable manner all or any of the time. This is absolutely contrary to all conventional physics. Newton's view of the universe as a machine is totally blown out of the window. The wave and particle conundrum of light illustrates this perfectly. Marcus Chown in his book *Quantum Theory Cannot Hurt You* gives the example of light passing through a window. When light hits the glass of a window 95% of it passes through. Five per cent of it is reflected back. This makes sense if light is a wave. Any wave hitting an obstruction will have part of itself carrying on and some bouncing back. If light is just a stream of particles then the problem is that the particles are identical. Why do some go back and some pass through? If they are identical particles they should be affected by the glass in the same way. The truth is that at this level identical individual particles cannot be always expected to behave in the same way. All we can say is that they have a chance of behaving the same way. There is no way of predicting which individual photon will move through the glass or be, like part of a wave, reflected back.

Life at the quantum level is thus inherently unpredictable. Even more strangely, for instance, rather than being 50-50 in the window situation, the probability is always 95-5. This is known as the probability wave. Although we cannot see each photon acting as both a particle and a wave at the same time, each photon has simultaneous wave and particle-like tendency. The particle nature of the photon must be informed how to behave by the wave side of its nature and vice versa. For mere mortals like us this is very difficult to grasp. The bottom line is that at these microscopic levels matter is fundamentally unpredictable. The sometimes wave-like behaviour, however, opens up other phenomena which are even weirder and more difficult to grasp.

The double slit experiment

To illustrate this wave characteristic of particles there is a famous trial called the double slit experiment. As I understand it, it works as follows: a stream of single photons are beamed towards a metal slab with two slits in it. A screen behind it is covered with sensitive light detectors. The detectors are supposed to register when the photons pass through the slits and hit the screen. Surprisingly a strange pattern was found registering on the detectors. This showed that some unexpected interference was occurring when a single photon was travelling through the slit on its own. If a larger beam of light was shone though the slits it registered a pattern of stripes, due to its wave-like nature. A stream of single photons should have registered two stripes only as they went through either slit. Yet a single photon registered the wave form. This could only mean that the photon, with its wave-like side, was going through both slits at the same time. The same experiment can be done with atoms or any microscopic particle.

This does sound unlikely, but another strange phenomenon was illustrated by the double slit experiment. When scientists were observing the experiment, the photons behaved as Newtonian science would have expected. They went though only one of the slits at a time. When the experiment was left to run unobserved, the wave form result began to occur. Somehow, observing things changed them.

Superpositions

It is a characteristic of waves that any one wave may be a combination of other currents and ripples but still be one wave. A large wave may have smaller waves on top, or ripples. These combinations of waves, being many but also one individual wave at the same time, are called superpositions.

Photons, and indeed all particles, can be waves. Their superpositions mean that in theory they may be in two (or multiple) places at once. Waves flow in the peaks and troughs that we observe in our common or garden seaside waves. If another set of waves interacts with an existing set of waves one of two things will happen. If the peaks and troughs are in phase they will just amalgamate. If the peaks correspond to the troughs and vice versa the waves will suffer from interference and seem to be cancelled out. The point is that in superpositions all possible combinations exist at the same time. Waves also seem to be able to do things that particles cannot. They can get places that a stream of particles could never reach. They can jump seemingly unbridgeable gaps, spread out really wide and so on. Science then concluded that the wave function of the fundamental particles allows superpositions. This means, in theory, that all matter could be in many places simultaneously. This may be possibly even in different dimensions.

Several places at once?

Does that mean that we can, in theory, be in more than one place at once? Well, we do not seem to be in our reality, but that is not to say that we may be also existing in another dimension or universe, as per the multiverse theory. According to quantum science this may be possible. What is actually to stop us acting as a wave? What is to stop us being in two or multiple places at once?

This should be likely in practice, as the potential for superposition exists theoretically with all the quantum particles that make up our atomic structure, when they are in their wave form.

All forms at once?

This is bad enough, but then things get more complicated. The quantum theory goes that all matter exists in all possible states. When ever it changes form, a particle instantaneously exists in all the possible states that it could hold. It only settles in its final position when someone observes it or measures it. Thought through, this is an amazing concept. Does this explain the strange changes in the double slit experiment? Why could our observation fix reality? Could this mean that our consciousness actually helps define what is around us? Reality suddenly seems more fragile.

Heisenberg's uncertainty principle

Another similar, but strange, concept governing our microscopic quantum world is the Heisenberg uncertainty principle. This is the very strange concept developed by Werner Heisenberg that states that all particles are forever in ceaseless motion, but we cannot measure both the velocity and position of any particle. We can measure its velocity and not be sure of its position or we can observe its position and not be sure of its velocity. This seems to be as a function of its wave/particle nature. This means that nothing in reality is actually fixed.

Entanglement

There is an even spookier inter-connectedness. That concerns something called entanglement.

Entanglement is the theory that once any particles interact with each other they are always somehow linked. If properties exhibited by one change then this affects the properties of all that have been interlinked.

Non-locality

The big brother of this is non-locality. This states that if particles are created together (as in a pair of electrons) any changes to one will instantaneously affect the other. For instance, if one electron spins one way and one the other, any changes in the spin of one will instantaneously affect the other. This will happen wherever both electrons end up. Even if they are separated by billions of light years in distance, it will still occur.

The consequences of this are enormous. As all matter was together and interacting at the time of the Big Bang, all particles, all being, must in some way be entangled. Our universe, with its quantum uncertainties, becomes a web of criss-crossed entanglements. We are all interconnected with all of creation and each other.

Zero point field

There is another sort of entanglement in our universe. This is called zero point field.

At school we were told that the vastness of empty space around us was a vacuum. This was never true; for more than forty years it has been known that the spaces between everything are filled with minute particles of energy/matter flashing in and out of existence in a split second. The temporary nature of this would of course make it difficult to detect, but its effects can be seen.

For instance, electrons are in continual motion around the nucleus of every atom. Negatively charged electrons ceaselessly orbit the positively charged nucleus. This movement requires energy. If electrons are losing energy in their progress, why are they not falling into the nucleus? Why does the positively charged nucleus not pull the electrons into the centre and collapse the atom? This, of course, would have catastrophic consequences for all of creation, and would take only a fraction of a second. The answer is that the energy from the zero point field replenishes any lost energy and maintains the *status quo* of the atoms.

More interestingly still, this fluctuating energy is measurable. Physicists have long allowed for it in their calculations without necessarily asking what it actually meant to the understanding of the true nature of things. The truth is that all of known existence is actually contained in this quantum field of energy. We are living in a web of light, like a gigantic force field, and are all interconnected within this quantum field.

Possibilities and a fixed world

The theories of quantum mechanics reveal a very strange world of possibilities. Nothing is certain, nothing can really be pinned down and all reality is interconnected. Matter can exist in all possible states at once and only settle on a final state when observed. Yet as we go about our lives the world around us seems solid and stable and separate. As matter bonds together in different combinations to form our world and us, no quantum behaviour can be observed. We still seem to be us in one place, one dimension, one time. Trees are trees, cars are cars, nothing seems to exhibit any of the strange things that would indicate the true shifting randomness of the universe's construction. The universe does seem to follow the machine-like rules identified all those years ago by Isaac Newton. How can that be?

The quantum puzzle

This is a very difficult question. Quantum mechanics are supposed to underpin all of existence. There seems to be no evidence of this in everyday life. There is of course some sort of explanation scientifically.

Strangely, one key seems to be that quantum events can never be observed directly. We can only observe the consequences. For instance, the wave-like form of particles can be understood via the double slit experiment, but not if it is being observed. Also zero point field can be detected only as the fluctuation in energy that has to be allowed for in other physics equations. We cannot see the superpositions of the atoms around us. We are not particularly aware of existing in more than one dimension. The interconnectedness of all of the universe seems generally to pass us by. But at the same time, we know that all we understand of the world, all we can understand of the world, is filtered and interpreted through our brains and minds. Our eyes work because of the stream of photons which are light hitting the cones and rods at the back of our retinas. This is translated into seeing by our brains. Our brains translate this sight into the everyday objects and things which make up our world. We see only through our minds. The interpretation of what we see cannot be separated from the mind of the observer. That is us as individuals.

Why do our minds not see the consequences of living in a quantum world? There are some possible explanations,

- It could be that matter, when forming the relatively 'solid' stuff like planets and people, exists as relatively dense clumps of atoms in combination. The many quantum probability waves may tend to cancel each other out and one reality, one set of probabilities, dominate.

- The set of superpositions fixes into one position on observation by us. The atoms and electrons that we are all made of choose a final state, and we and the world that we are observing around us seem stable and fixed.

- It could also be that our minds do see the quantum chaos around us and decide on what reality should be fixed. This may be done on an individual basis, or we may construct an agreed reality as a co-operative venture.

- Or, of course, a creator may decide our version of reality for us.

Quantum mechanics does however give possibilities of mechanisms within science for some of the phenomena considered weird and unscientific now. For instance, can some people instinctively see other dimensions within the quantum field? Is telepathy just a result of entanglement? Has the future already happened and some people can read that? Are some people picking up information via the inter-connectedness of things? Are there other levels of reality that interact with ours?

Even with the rigours of the advanced scientific methods of quantum mechanics, the questions generated concerning the true nature of our reality go on and on. In many ways we are back where we started over two thousand years ago. For all our scientific knowledge, we are essentially no further on in understanding the nature of the universe. High science seems to be posing more questions than it has answers for. Especially in this study of fundamental particles, the possibilities for the truth of reality seem to be opening up, not closing down.

Aspects of reality

- On a quantum level, fundamental particles do not obey the machine theories of Isaac Newton, which underpin the classical physics of our universe.

- The behaviour of any individual particle cannot be predicted.

- All fundamental particles which make up the universe can act either as particles or waves.

- Waves can do things particles cannot. They can spread over vast distances. They can hold superpositions.

- On changing form, all particles hold all possible positions simultaneously. They only fix into a final position when someone observes them.

- All particles are in perpetual motion.

- All particles that make up the universe are fundamentally entangled.

- Space is not a vacuum, but a quantum sea of light, as per zero point field.

The strangeness of Quantum Mechanics reveals a more uncertain reality than is usually proposed by science. If they are sound, the reflections of reality generated by these theories have made things more complicated, not easier. For instance, could we be fixing reality ourselves? Is it being fixed for us?

To try and make further sense of things, I went back again to the only hard evidence we have, that is ourselves and our human bodies.

CHAPTER THIRTEEN

Back to basics: healing

The more I thought about and researched possibilities of where we came from and what creatures we actually were, the more that the impossibilities of finding any definite answers became obvious. Which aspects of reality were most likely? In looking for clues to the big picture of reality, the questions posed are not only too big, but are, in essence, beyond our current understanding of science or cosmology to answer. Who are we? Where do we really come from? How did we get to be here? What is our true nature? Who do we think we are anyway?? The same unanswerable questions keep going round and round.

Beyond the cutting edge physics and cosmology (which may be superseded with something quite different in a few years) I thought again perhaps that the only definite clues that we have before us may be in looking carefully at ourselves. We, in our own physical human bodies, may be the best clues we have.

Could we actually be evolutionary accidents, results of chance evolution, as biological science may say? Or are we something quite different, as some alternative thinkers hold to be true? We have to look for the anomalies, things that happen with the human body which, if the accepted theories of humanity only as biological beings were accurate, should not be possible. I did this by looking at what happens when the human body malfunctions. In looking at how these malfunctions can be corrected, by using particular alternative methods of healing, it became very obvious that humanity as only biological beings could not be the whole story.

The human body

The human body is a very complex biological machine. As already mentioned, probably too complex to have evolved by total accident. Even though the human body seems well designed, it does often malfunction. There are several ways in which the body stops working properly. In looking at these, and how the malfunctions are corrected using alternative means, interesting insights into different sorts of reality are exposed.

Malfunction

There are several different ways in which the human body can go wrong.

Firstly, any of the internal systems can get out of balance or malfunction. They can simply stop working properly or become damaged or diseased. For example, kidney failure or thyroid malfunction. These can make a person feel ill or even, in extreme cases, cause them to sicken and die. Organs, like the heart, can be or become faulty. If the blood cannot pump oxygen around and waste cannot be eliminated a person may become very sick indeed. Arteries may become clogged and blocked so blood cannot flow freely. Drugs and medicines have been developed which may help to alleviate or put things right, but it is not always wholly possible.

Secondly, and I simplify, the numerous different types of cells from which our bodies are constructed reproduce themselves continually. Sometimes they make mistakes and start reproducing the faulty cells. These rogue, or cancerous cells, can devastate internal organs, and may cause sickness and death, especially when they spread throughout the body. Conventional treatment involves surgery, to remove the growth if possible. It also may involve radio- or chemotherapy. Radio-therapy burns the offending tissues away and chemotherapy poisons the cancerous tissues. Both can take a terrible toll on the body and the healthy tissues around.

Thirdly, accident. Trauma can cause injury and death. Severe shock can actually kill. Loss of blood can cause real problems. Loss of or damage to a major internal organ can kill or seriously impair.

Luckily we have doctors and surgeons who can sometimes do wonderful repair work.

Fourthly, infectious disease. Our bodies can be invaded by the small, microscopic forms of life that in fact are some of the oldest life on earth. Their ancestors are thought to be much older than man. These are bacteria or viruses. They survive and reproduce by entering a host human body and taking over cells and then massively replicating themselves. This causes a range of illnesses, some minor, some life threatening.

The human body has a relatively efficient immune system. Special killer cells will try to seek out and destroy any strange or hostile organisms that enter the bloodstream. Disease will occur when this process is inefficient or the organism is new and the body has not met it before and has no immunity. There is very little that can be done for a viral infection. The body may heat itself up to a high temperature to kill the organisms. Some antibiotics may make a little difference. However, with bacterial infections antibiotics are more effective. In healthy humans, most infections will recover in a reasonable time on their own, providing reasonable rest and fluids are taken.

Illness and evolution

It seems that so much could go wrong which would make humanity non-viable. The truth is that most beings, if they have enough food and are not felled by accident or disease, seem to cope with the hazards and survive. It has to be asked, what is the role of illness? Why do we actually get ill? If we think we are just biological creatures of random evolution, then sickness can be seen to have a role in this process. It actually has a purpose.

In the big biological picture, viruses and bacteria are just primitive life forms which actually predate our evolution. Sickness generated from them is just a by-product of their needing to replicate. It is worth noting though that the intention is not necessarily to kill the hosts, as that would be a very inefficient way of reproducing themselves. Some biologists think that they have a function in evolution. As they tend to kill the weaker host, the stronger will tend to survive and breed.

This also enables the food chain to function better, especially in the sea. They have a logical role in evolutionary process in eliminating the weaker elements of all animals, including man. If the weaker people and animals die more easily through illness then they are less likely to breed. The stronger genes are more likely then to be carried forward into improving the race or species. Weaker animals are more likely also to become the food source for those higher up the food chain.

Those with illnesses, such as cancer, can be seen as just unfortunate victims of malfunctioning cell replication, whatever the external or internal cause. Accidents are just accidents, the fittest will also have a better chance of surviving them. Those with illnesses which are caused by imbalance of the complex systems of the body could just be seen as unlucky. Then again, it could be seen as an evolutionary tool. Those with better balanced systems are more likely to thrive and breed. Sickness then could be seen just as nature's way of ensuring efficient food chains and a stronger breeding population.

Not the whole story

The point is, though, if we are really only biological beings, then only the mechanical conventional medicines and those techniques that assume we are, should be effective in putting right the bodily malfunctions. This does not always seem to be true. There have always been those in society that have healed the human body without the conventional medicines and means.

Biology plus

Could there be an extra ingredient, or ingredients, to the humanity make up which allows these other means of healing to work? It may be that there are some non-physical dimensions to the body which help and enable this. It also opens up the possibility for there being other methods of healing or diagnosing malfunctions in the human body. These could give us clues to other dimensions to humanity, not understood by the disciplines of conventional medicines and our mechanical understandings of the human body.

In practice there are many clues to these alternatives there. Some are scientific, some clues are only anecdotal. The body of evidence is growing and growing, though. The biological body can be shown not to be the whole story.

Body repair

At the moment we need doctors and surgeons to do mechanical tasks, like setting broken limbs or doing major heart surgery or issuing drugs or antibiotics. They diagnose by listening to symptoms or doing tests, using their training and experience. They treat conventionally and efficiently. The fact that such a complex machine actually manages to function reasonably most of the time is accepted. It is amazing, when you think about it, that it works most of the time. That this fact is almost miraculous seems to pass most of us by.

Along side the 'mechanical' doctors there are many many people who consider themselves healers. They have a different view of the human body, and how to repair and heal it. With this, implicitly, comes an different understanding of the true nature of humanity. If the human body was just brute biology, a random product of evolution only, other methods of healing simply would not work. There is, in fact, massive anecdotal evidence and some scientific that at least some of them do.

An alternative view of the human body

It is in looking at these bodily malfunctions and how they are repaired that the reflections of strange alternative realities seem strongest. What is indicated most of all is that the human body is multi-layered. It has both a physical biological and an energy body also. It also contains a system of so-called energy meridians. This is not only a modern view. Ancient wisdom has often assumed as much.

If you remember, the components that make up our body are, after all, also themselves made of the vibrating energies of our atomic structure. The theory is that there are other layers of energy also. It is these (including the so-called subtle body) that lend an external hand in ensuring that the systems of our complex, interacting physical bodies work properly together. Furthermore, in fact, the mind can also be seen to have an important role in healing and repairing the human body.

Healing

Healing is a method of putting right the body imbalances and restoring health, without conventional medicines. If the physical biological body was all that there was to humanity, then this healing would not work.

Alongside the medical scientists there have always been healers. Strangely, there is growing medical support for disciplines like acupuncture and shiatsu which work on so-called energy meridians of the body. There has also been some level of acceptance for homeopathy. These have often been dismissed as nonsense by conventional medicine yet seem to be effective in some cases.

The Eastern cultures have long had traditions of healing, often using methods other than those which we consider conventional. There have always been followings for herbalists with their potions, wise men and of course shamans and witch doctors. There have been hands-on healers, spiritual healers and of course factions of the Church of England which believe that God will cure or heal if asked. Alongside this there are the 'New Age' healers who often see auras and claim to work with energy to heal and re-balance the human (or animal in some cases) body. There seem to be several different ways to do this. If this healing is actually possible then how. What does it say about the true nature of mankind? Each type of healing gives us some clues to, or reflections of, different possible realities.

As stated before, the human body is a cell-based, organic structure. This structure can be prone to malfunction. It can also be subject to disease and decay. If we were just biological beings, only conventional medicine, which is drug based, would be useful in rectifying any malfunctions. The truth is though that there are many methods of healing these bodies that illustrate and utilize forces beyond those of the purely physical world.

Types of healing

I have identified four main types of healing that do this, and there may be more.

- There are those who believe, as we are created by God, or an intelligent designer, that he can heal us or empower others to heal us in his name. There is a long tradition in our culture of people who believe this does happen.

- There are those who believe that the mind can be used to heal the physical body, either by external or internal means. Similarly there are cults like voodoo which maintain the reverse to be true: that you can make someone ill because they believe you are able to.

- We are physical beings made of energy, living in an energy matrix. Some believe that outside energy can be used to re-tune the body and correct any imbalances.

- It is also accepted in most healing circles that we all have an energy body which lives in harmony with our physical body. This can be re-tuned in several ways to enable the body to heal itself.

All these healing methods may say something about the possibilities of different realities that may make up our universe. There is some evidence for all of them.

Firstly, healing using a divine creative force

If we have a God or universal creator, who has at some point designed the human race, then he should be able to repair any damage to his creations and heal if he chooses to. If this were possible it would indicate very strongly that we are not just biological beings. Historically this, anecdotally at least in the Christian tradition, and in many other cultures, has been seen to have been done in some form for hundreds of years. The concept of healing with a divine intervention seems to have a lot of credence in some sections of our culture.

Evidence of religious healing

For instance, our Christian Holy Bible refers explicitly to Jesus, the son of God, healing.

"When the sun was setting, the people brought to Jesus all who had various kinds of sickness, and laying his hands on each one, he healed them". Luke 4.40

Healing has also since then been done, with prayer, in his name. The New Testament of the Christian Bible has many other examples of Jesus healing.

There are many people in mainstream religion, including the Church of England, who believe such healing is still possible today. My own local vicar believes strongly that it is possible to ask for healing through prayer and receive it. He quoted two examples from his personal experience. One involved help for an asthmatic youth, and the other involved bones resetting themselves through prayer. When I questioned whether it was not just the power of their collective minds triggering the healing, the response was that the bodies were regenerating at speeds that were not possible naturally.

Lourdes

Belief in miraculous healing is especially true of the Catholic church. There is, of course, the veritable industry involved in the healing power of some earthly sites, for instance like the town of Lourdes in France. People travel there supposedly both to feel closer to God and to receive healing. This site, which was said to have been visited by the Virgin Mary, has a grotto and healing waters from a spring. Things began when the Virgin Mary was said to have appeared to 14 year old girl, Bernadette, many times in the late nineteenth century. A spring appeared at the spot where she had been seen, which began to be known for its miraculous healing properties. It became a place of pilgrimage. Thousands and thousands of tourists and pilgrims visit annually to receive a blessing or healing from the holy spring. There are reportedly many cases of healing that can be verified every year. Many of the sick report that they have a small (not necessarily miraculous) but beneficial improvement in their ailments after visiting. A recent newspaper article about Lourdes mentioned that there had been at least 200 million visitors in the last 152 years and at least 67 miracle healings that the Catholic church had officially recognized.

Indeed, this was witnessed by a modern day pilgrim to Lourdes via the Jumbulance Trust. The Jumbulance regularly takes very sick people to Lourdes and other pilgrim sites for healing with a contingent of able-bodied helpers. One such helper, Roy Gregory, wrote about his experiences in October 2008. He witnessed for himself the increase in well-being of his charges, mentally and physically. He also felt that, with the contingent of the sick and their helpers "We experienced God through Lourdes, the grandeur of the Pyrenees and each other".

Whether the healing is all in the mind or not, the very high proportion of religious personnel (nuns, priests, etc) that I saw there shows that there is a strong belief both in miracles and healing in the general run of Christian, especially Catholic, churches. There are of course other such sites of pilgrimage and healing all over the world.

The difficult question

The question has to be asked, however, if we are created by God, and are not just biological beings, what role has illness? Why allow such suffering? The only answer I have been given is that we cannot know the mind of God. There will be a reason, but we are not allowed to know it. One reason given historically is that in sickness and disaster we are brought closer to a realization of God. We become aware of ourselves as not just physical biological beings. The fact that it seems possible to heal using divine intervention, does increase the likelihood of there being a divinity of some sort in our reality. It may also just show us how powerful the human mind can be, though.

Secondly, healing with the mind

The human mind is a very powerful machine. Scientists still do not know exactly how it works. There are still many mysteries which are not yet solved or fully understood. To recap, there is the conscious mind with which we are aware, and the subconscious mind which is also vast and powerful. Our thoughts, biologically, can be seen as just biochemical energy. When we talk or think we are putting energy out into the energy matrix which surrounds us. This energy is forever buzzing. Also we are not consciously aware of the many functions with which the mind co-ordinates our physical body. These are continually at work even whilst we are asleep. There are thus three main possibilities when discussing whether healing with the mind is possible:

- It may be that the part of the mind which co-ordinates and regulates our body can be encouraged to independently 'tune up' our natural immune system.

- It may be that the conscious part of our mind can instruct our sub-consciousness to do the same, or vice versa.

- Perhaps even the vibrational energy from our thoughts and words can somehow tune up the very fabric of our being.

If we are not just biological beings, the possibilities may be endless. This may be especially true if our mind is not just the biochemical flow of firing neurons, but something extra as well.

The placebo effect

Is there any evidence for any of the above possibilities? Can the mind heal? There is in fact a long acknowledged phenomenon that seems to indicate this. This is the so-called placebo effect. The placebo effect means that because we think that we are being treated for an ailment, we actually feel or get better, whether we are actually receiving the drugs that we think we are being given or not. For instance, if someone is given pills for a condition and they believe these to be genuine, but they are in fact only sugar pills, there is often an improvement. This is often widely accepted by the medical profession and yet what it actually means in the big picture is dismissed. I even saw a documentary on TV long ago when people thought they had had surgery done on painful knees. In fact they had just been opened up and then closed without any work being done.

There was actually improvement in some cases. The mind thought that the body was being repaired and the pain alleviated, therefore it was. Is this partly what may be happening in Lourdes?

Immune system override

When discussing mind over matter it is worth mentioning how our health is affected by the state of our body's immune system. This is our first line of defence from infectious disease. For years there was a so-called 'old wives' tale' that the individual's immune system was affected by their mental state. That meant if people were stressed or low they were more likely to suffer a poor immune system and catch more colds, coughs or more serious ailments.

This fact was strenuously denied by the medical and scientific professions as they could see no physical link. As I understand it, data collected for cancer survival rates revealed, surprisingly, that there did seem to be a correlation. Those with a more positive attitude seemed to survive longer. Eventually, of course, they did find an endocrinal link. The state of emotions could be seen to trigger a glandular response in the body that tuned-up or suppressed the immune system. The mind was overriding the physical body, albeit unconsciously. If you believed that you were going to get better, there was more chance that you would. Or vice versa.

The truth is that our mind is seemingly capable of instigating improvements in the body without conventional help. Is this always just the mind stimulating the body's natural defence systems? This may be just a biological, natural process. Or is it another sort of proof that the biological body is not the whole story? It may be an indication that the physical body is just part of a bigger picture that we do not yet quite understand.

Thirdly, healing with the energy matrix

We are, as mentioned before, beings made from the atomic energy of the substances that make up our physical bodies. We are in fact energy beings living in an energy matrix. Our earth abounds with measurable energies, such as its magnetic and gravitational fields, heat and light and x-ray to name just a few. There are also even fields such as the ley lines which are more controversial, but detectable by some people. These are lines of energy running thoughout the earth which cannot be detected yet scientifically, but can be located by dowsing. This can be done using rods or a pendulum. There is a long history of successful dowsing in our culture. For example, country-men have always been able to dowse for water, detecting the change in energies with rods or even two twigs. They have been using the energy matrix to find what they have been looking for. As David Furlong explains in his book *Earth Energies*:

"Electromagnetic fields weave through the physical world in a seamless web connecting particle to particle. These energy fields surround all living things, creating slightly different matrices of energy depending on the organism in question."

The important thing to remember is that as human beings – as complex biological beings – we cannot actually function well without the electromagnetic fields that surround us on earth. When astronauts first went into space it was discovered that even after a relatively small period of time they lost bone mass and muscle tone once they were away from the physical earth. They now have magnets which generate electromagnetic fields within their space suits, to combat this.

As we are fundamentally made of energy, could it be scientifically possible to use outside energies to re-set any malfunctions? Perhaps in the future this could be scientifically possible. Many people routinely now also use magnets to aid healing. Some scientist somewhere is most certainly trying to create such a machine at this current point of time. Certainly they managed it on Star Trek!

The human energy body

Is there any evidence of any of this? Well, traces of one sort of body energy can be detected scientifically and can also be seen by some individuals. It can also be photographed, using special sensitive cameras. It can be seen as an egg-shaped layer of different coloured lights around the whole body. This is called the aura.

The aura

The aura is simply a layer of energies, of different wavelengths, surrounding the human body. All living things, in fact anything that has an atomic structure, will have some sort of aura. An aura is just the energy field generated around matter caused by the movement and vibration of the electrons, etc., that we, and everything around us, are made of. The human body is a complex machine that uses bioelectrical energy to run the brain and the nervous system and chemical exchange to run the blood and glandular systems. It takes in energy via food and converts it into the chemicals needed by various organs to operate. It generates heat whilst doing this. It is always working even when we are asleep. All this energy exchange is bound to leave discernible electronic traces.

Some people claim to be able to see these energy auras. They can see them as egg-shaped clouds around people. They see different colours within these auras. How is this possible and why do we not all see them if they exist? Some people's eyes are more sensitive to these energies than others. In the way that some people see colour slightly differently from others, due to the difference in the rods and cones in the back of their eyes, some people may be able to see these vibrations around us. It also, of course, depends on the individual visual decoding circuits in the brain. The auras appear coloured because colour is just the way our brains interpret different wavelengths of light. Some people just do not see them, or expect to see them, others do. Some do, but do not think they should be able to, so do not admit it. I recently spoke to a friend who mentioned casually that her own mother used to think that she had bad eyes because she could see colours around people. They vanished when she hit puberty at thirteen.

Asking around, it is very interesting how many friends and acquaintances admit to seeing some sort of aura around people. They have just learnt not to mention it in public!

The auras are said to extend into the space around us. We cannot really tell how far. The ancient masters were supposed to have vast auras which spread for miles. This is supposed to explain why they had such vast numbers of followers. They were attracted to the master by feeling the aura. When we are standing close to someone, or in a crowd, our auras touch or mingle. We are more sensitive to this than we realize. When someone is too close to us we feel that they are invading our personal space. We often like or dislike people at first acquaintance with out knowing why. The only way we can put it into words is by saying that our energies, or 'auras' are or are not compatible. It is said that a group of people whose energies are in harmony is much more effective than when the opposite is true, and will achieve more.

Traces of other energies of the body can also be detected within the aura. This is not scientifically measurable as yet. For instance, I have spoken to several people who state that they can sometimes see colours around someone that indicates their mood. As thoughts are bioenergy this must, I suppose, be possible. People, anyway, see what they see. Who is anyone to say that what you see is not possible? Many of us do suppress glimpses of any phenomena that do not fit in with what is considered mainstream.

It is also possible to feel auras. Some sensitive people claim to be able to feel the boundaries of auras. As they are some sort of electrical field this is entirely possible. I remember someone saying to me a long time ago, as they held their hands over me in a healing session "this is the edge of your aura". As they did it I had felt a tingling like a small electric shock. The evidence that auras exist is actually unanswerable.

Personal evidence

Have I personal evidence? Well I do not generally see auras, although if I concentrate I can see a slight electrical disturbance around people. Once though, when I was walking with friends on an ancient hill in Dorset, I turned around and suddenly saw this wonderful green and gold aura surrounding a passing stranger. It was a magnificent sight. As soon as I thought to my self "I can't see auras" it vanished and everything was as normal. I was not thinking of auras or expecting to see one at the time so I do not know where that vision suddenly came from. But I now know that they do exist. I felt very privileged to see it, though.

Small children, including my elder daughter as a small child, often see auras. She often mentioned a blue mist around myself and my late mother. They seem to lose the knack as they get older and understand that you should not. Our saints were always illustrated with halos (auras?) around their heads as an indication of holiness. The aura is apparently often stronger and more visible around the head. Highly sensitive cameras, like those operated in the film industry, will often accidentally pick up these colours surrounding people. It is actually possible to go to specialist photographer and have your photo taken. The resulting colours can be, in theory, analyzed. I had mine done in Glastonbury in 2004. I am shown being surrounded by an intense red aura with patches of gold. The handout that I was given states that this indicated certain things about me that were in fact roughly true (but could of course be generic). The gold was supposed to indicate someone who could be an inspiration to other people. This would explain, I suppose, why our saints had gold auras.

Auras and healing

Some practitioners also maintain that health state and wellbeing can be diagnosed by looking at the aura. The theory is that different colours or variations of strength of the aura can indicate an imbalance in the complex bodily systems. This can then be righted using spiritual healing of some sort.

Healing practice

How do people actually heal with these energies? There are several different ways of healing with the energy matrix. Some healers hold their hands just above or on the bodies of those being healed. Some people use hands on, and touch the part of the body that they think needs healing. They feel they either pull up electromagnetic energy from the energy of the earth matrix or pull down energy from a universal stream of energy. This universal stream of energy is said to originate either from a creator god, or from the general energy matrix. This energy is used to top up and replenish or re-balance the energy body which then can tune up the physical being.

Crystal and other alternative healing

There are other methods of healing which also use the fact that the very atoms of which we are made are themselves just different vibrating quanta (pinches of energy) in combination. As we are creatures of vibration, the vibrations can be re-harmonized, as in tuning a piano with a tuning fork. This can be done by sound or by use of appropriate crystals. The theory is that the crystals contain different vibrational rates which can re-tune the body where required. Crystals can be seen as reservoirs of stored energy of different vibrational frequency. Flower essence healing is done with the vibrational frequency of the flower constituents. These act on the human energy bodies to re-tune them or act on mood or the mental state. There may be many other examples also. Could this be an explanation for the mechanism of working of the scientifically much derided, but anecdotally very effective, homeopathy? Apparently even our Queen uses this, but as science at the moment cannot actually see how it works it is often still believed to be phoney.

Fourthly, healing with the subtle body

Many people believe that alongside our physical bodies there does exist an energetic body or bodies that actually power and regulate our physical bodies. That is our scientifically undetectable 'subtle' or spiritual energy body. It is different from the energy body that comes from our atomic structure. It can also be detected in the aura by those sensitive enough. The subtle body is a body made of spirit energy that works in combination with our physical body. It functions alongside the physical body (some even say that it is a blueprint). This holds our thoughts, emotions and of course our soul energy. Indeed the belief is that our purely physical body could not function with out it.

This subtle body is said to exist outside of time and space and is considered directly connected both to the earth and to any creator god. It is linked by something called the Hara, or energy channel, to this universal grid. It may be reflected in the deeper layers of our aura. It is this body that many healers feel that they are working with. Re-tuning of this subtle body enables the physical body to re-balance and work better. It can also allow the physical body to then fight infection or heal illness or wounds. It is held also that there is constant communication and interchange between the subtle and physical bodies. They actually work as one in practice. Some people feel that our thoughts and emotions can transfer from the subtle body to the physical and affect our health and vice versa. The theory is that every living thing will have a subtle body. It is an energy body, not detectable by science. Some people also believe that even non-living things may also have subtle bodies and may possibly have some form of rudimentary consciousness.

There is much about the subtle body in esoteric literature. Some mystics maintain that we have more than one, rising through the different dimensions in which we exist. This concept has been around for many thousands of years in many cultures, especially Eastern. There are many different variations of theories on its nature and what it actually consists of. Some people believe that we have layers of spirit bodies, some say seven, rising up to the divine. The consensus seems to be, though, that it is all aspects of ourselves that are not physical. This is our thoughts, emotions, and of course our soul/consciousness.

There is said to be constant movement between the two bodies, both ways. We can tune up, or negatively affect, our subtle bodies by what we eat, drink or think or feel. For instance too many stimulants (including alcohol, tea and coffee, let alone drugs) can cause all sorts of trouble. Positive thinking and meditation can help our physical bodies to re-balance.

The energy matrix in which our physical bodies exist, is at least somewhat measurable. The subtle energies that many think run parallel to that body are not detectable, at least with science at the stage it is now. This does not mean to say they do not exist though. Indeed there is strong anecdotal evidence spanning thousands of years that they may do so. If they did not, then the forms of healing mentioned next could simply not happen.

Healing with aspects of the subtle body

There are forms of healing which are said to work with those aspects of the subtle bodies which are seemingly embedded within the physical body. These are the so-called chakras and meridians. This include some popular, more seemingly mainstream, disciplines such as reflexology and acupuncture.

Healing using Chakras

There are many healers these days who believe that it is possible to heal using these. They are the revolving vortices of energy that are said to power our subtle energy body, and thus our physical body. They are literally energy wheels; chakra means wheel in Sanskrit.

The theory is that the human body is so complex, and needs so much energy to function, that it has to pull in energy from the universe to survive and thrive. It does this using chakras. The concept of chakras has been around in various forms for thousands of years. These constantly spinning wheels of energy, seemingly deeply embedded in the physical body, spin continually, some clockwise, some the reverse. The main ones run down the human body in a straight line. They correspond to the important glands in the physical body. More controversially even, they can be seen to coincide with important plexus points, or networks of nerves. They run from crown via third eye to base. They have names such as Crown Chakra, Heart Chakra etc.

The resultant energies can be detected by sensitive practitioners physically feeling the energies, or by use of pendulums. Some people claim to be able to see them. If you hold a crystal on a chain or string above the certain points on your body it will rotate as it gets caught up with the energies circling from them. I can actually detect these on myself. They may get out of balance, or almost shut down. A practitioner will heal, by hand or crystal, balancing and evening up the chakras. They will ensure that they are all doing their job with the energies flowing freely.

Balanced chakras mean a balanced body physically and spiritually. Yoga is a way of achieving this. As we are dealing with the subtle body energies, their existence cannot be 'proved' scientifically. There is however, as mentioned before, overwhelming anecdotal evidence that they do exist and people have been working with them for thousands of years, especially in eastern ancient cultures. Some people go even further and say that there are chakras, powering wheels, throughout the natural world, including the planet itself.

Healing using meridians

There is another type of energy system which is said to also be embedded in the physical body which healers, and acupuncturists in particular, use. Acupuncture deals with unseen energy flows through the human body, along pathways which are called meridians. These energy meridians form a grid around the human body. There are twelve main meridians, half ying and half yang. The theory goes that for optimum health, the life force (subtle body?) or qi must be allowed to flow evenly around the body. Disruption on any point on a meridian can cause illness at any point along it. For instance the stomach meridian also passes though the upper gums. A problem in the stomach could cause toothache. Any imbalance of the yin/yang balance causes problems. Malfunctioning glands or organs can inhibit this. Fine needles are inserted into points corresponding to the meridians on which the malfunctioning organ also resides. This re-balances the energies of the meridian. This tunes up the organs along that meridian, and relieves pain. There seems much more general acceptance in our culture, than there is for other alternative practices, that acupuncture works. This is particularly true for problems that mainstream medicine cannot always cope with, especially pain relief.

There is apparently some sort of a body of scientific evidence to support the use of acupuncture in treating certain ailments. There are many theories abounding as to why it works. Many scientists believe it works by stimulating natural endorphins to block pain. There is also considerable anecdotal evidence that it works well for things like depression and addiction.

However it works, the bottom line is that Western doctors are now understanding more and more that acupuncture healing does have an effect on the human body. It seems particularly useful in cases where western medicine does not have all of the answers, like pain relief. Acupressure and Shiatsu also use these energy meridians to heal, often very successfully. Reflexology, which uses points on the meridians, some of which coincide with those used in acupuncture, which exist on the feet and hands, is also another therapy which is becoming more successful and respectable in our western culture. This re-balances the body by pressure on the appropriate spot on the feet corresponding to the body part for the organ that is malfunctioning or system that is not functioning properly.

Does healing work?

Anecdotally and practically it seems that it does. Personally I can testify that it has worked for me. Many people make a living from healing, which they could not if it was not at least partially successful. There have always been stories of miracle cures and individual successful healings. There is more and more recognition within our culture that the physical body is not the whole story.

Aspects of reality

- The human body can malfunction. These malfunctions can be put right with methods that do not include conventional drug-based methods.

- Healing can be shown to happen using the power of the human mind.

- Healing can be shown to happen using a divine creative force.

- Our bodies are made from vibrating energy.

- We are energy beings living in an energy matrix.

- The energy body can be detected in our aura.

- Healing can be done using methods including crystal healing to re-tune the vibrations and maximize health and well being.

- Healing can be shown to happen using a universal energy source from within the matrix.

- Humanity has a spiritual energy, or subtle, body.

- This spiritual, or subtle, body works in harmony with the physical body.

- It is said to be connected to the universal energy source by the Hara.

- Healing can be shown to happen using the spiritual energy body.

- The spiritual body reveals itself in the meridians and chakras embedded in the physical body.

- The fact that these unconventional methods of healing work indicates the presence of aspects of reality beyond those of humanity as just biological beings.

Personally, I found that the most interesting aspect of reality I looked at in all this, was that the human mind can be shown to have the power to persuade the human body to reset or heal itself. What does it say about us and the nature of our minds if we can use them to heal? This again throws up the mystery of the nature of our consciousness and its effect on our reality.

Does this study of healing prove that the aspects of reality which they rely on to work, do exist? That is, of course, with our limited technology, unprovable. What it does say though is that something else beyond our merely obvious physical bodies is happening. The anomalies are there that prove we are not yet able to understand the whole story of reality. We simply cannot be just the purely biological beings that we think we are. This indicates that there is a different big picture of reality in existence, than that which we have been taught is going on in the universe. We can say that the existence of successful healing, beyond medical science, 'proves' that the mainstream theory of reality of man as only a creature of biology can be shown to be flawed at best.

To try to clarify things further, I next look at the other anomalies in our system, which if true would indicate a different actual reality from that which we have all grown up with. I looked at those people who see the future, and those other people who have skills beyond those which merely biological beings could expect to have.

CHAPTER FOURTEEN

Curiouser and curiouser:
the strange skills of the human mind..

In looking back at the reality of our human biology, and the various ways of correcting malfunctions, glimpses of other interesting aspects of reality began to show themselves. Once you begin to look up from the mainstream, the true nature of reality seems both more complicated and more mysterious than we have been led to believe.

Some people see the universe to be a multi-layered, multi-dimensional entity, either randomly occurring or designed by someone or something. Others see it as something bigger and more complex and even more peculiar than science could ever allow. However, nothing points out the limits of the conventional Newtonian (universe as a rational machine) view more than those exceptions and anomalies that do exist within our society, and that science dismisses as unprovable experimentally, therefore hocus pocus. These exceptions do prove (or test) the rule.

Exceptions

As well as the documented ability of the human mind to aid in healing the human body, there is another whole interesting raft of exceptions to be found in our society. All of these point to different possible aspects of reality. In this chapter I look at some of these that concern special gifts or abilities that some people have. These abilities simply should not exist if we are only biological beings living on a randomly formed planet. For instance, some people seem to see the future. Some people seem able to communicate without words, sometimes over vast distances. Some people seem to alter what may happen in the future by magic or prayer. For some of these, there are the possibilities within quantum mechanics of future rational explanations. However, some phenomena do indicate quite powerfully that the Newtonian universe cannot possibly be the whole story. It is these aspects in particular that I felt needed investigation. I asked myself which aspect of reality could they 'prove' to be most likely true?

Even within conventional society, we have all heard of the strange gifts and powers that some people seem to have. They have skills that seem to defy rational explanation. As I have progressed through life I have met and spoken to more and more people who have experienced or practised these alternative skills. Some people do claim to be able to see the future or read minds.

The power of the human mind

Phenomena such as mind reading and soothsaying or even magic have a long history in many cultures, including to an extent our own. The ancients took these things very seriously. They are sometimes also taken very seriously now in modern times, in unexpected quarters. Some people even believe that you can change the future by prayer or spells or by the power of thought.

Skills of the ancients

There is a long history both in our culture, and in many older cultures throughout the ages, of some people having, or claiming to have, these gifts. From the village witch, including and up to the court astrologers, these soothsayers, or oracles, seem to have been taken seriously in the ancient world, in some cases by the establishment as well as the common people. Often they would use incense, meditative or mind-altering methods to lift the mind onto a higher plane to enable them to do this. Throughout history, seers and oracles, or just wise women, would pronounce on outcomes and future events when requested. Sometimes even princes and kings would consult them at tricky times. In Tudor times, for instance, there were wandering psychics and even court astrologers consulted by the monarchs and noblemen routinely. Although now not mainstream, there are many today in all levels of society who understand that some individuals can sometimes see glimpses into the future, without questioning how it is possible. Just because science cannot yet see a mechanism, this does not mean that it is not possible, especially since the anecdotal evidence is often so strong.

Modern times

Today many practitioners also use methods to raise their minds to a higher level to tap into universal forces. Sometimes they feel they are connecting with the gods or angels, sometimes with a universal creator, sometimes just with the earth energies or higher realms. Some people just use the power of their minds. Most practitioners today also often seem to use objects as props or indicating symbols. The topic is very involved and complicated. What follows are a few examples from my own research and experience.

Telepathy

The phenomenon of telepathy has a long history of quasi-acceptance in certain sections of society. Telepathy is said to happen when people's thoughts, feelings and emotions seem to be communicated across distance. It seems to occur particularly when people have an emotional bond or connection with those communicated with. This includes siblings, parents and children and even pets and owners. Some, such as the telepathy between twins, has been well documented. There are even cases when a twin has bruised themselves and their other twin comes out in an identical bruise even when they are many miles away. It seems quite a common tale that when one twin is hurt or in danger the other knows instantly. Interestingly a friend reported to me that her husband's twin used to communicate with his identical brother, without using spoken language, as a small child. To a lesser extent, many of us can give minor examples of telepathy. These include incidents such as knowing who is calling when the phone rings, or thinking of someone and that person contacting you the same day. It may seem trivial but it does indicate that information, thoughts, or even intentions to ring are reaching across the seemingly empty air.

Some people do seem more attuned to picking up others' thoughts and feelings than others. It would of course make living very difficult it we all knew what each other was thinking the whole time!! Experiments have been tried in laboratory conditions, attempting to transmit images from one person to another. The results have not generally been conclusive, although often above that achieved by pure chance.

It is worth noting, though, that sometimes some people are just very sensitive and naturally intuitive and may pick up others' emotions and feelings using these tools. Also, as you may remember, our senses are picking up information all the time and from all sources. We are not always aware of this as we would be swamped. Our computer like brains screen out most of the information and we are conscious only of that which we need to cope with everyday life. Sometimes when we feel something is not quite right it is because our subconscious has picked up natural signals that our conscious brain is not aware of.

There is also the well known subject of close animals, such as cats and dogs and even horses having some sort of psychic bond with their owners and seemingly anticipating their needs, or on a basic level, knowing when they are coming home after being away for a time. Some people do seem to have bonds with animals which allow communication without words. So-called horse whispering and dog whispering, communication with troubled animals to find out what is the matter with them, is used more and more.

Possible mechanism for telepathy

If you believe that telepathy does exist, what could be a possible mechanism for it to work? As you may remember, thoughts and emotions are, in their basic form, only biochemical energy generated in the brain. Energy, after all, can be transmitted outwards, and be picked up by those with receptive brains. There could then indeed be a case for thoughts travelling across the energy matrix and being somehow picked up by close friends or relatives that we are attuned to. As you may remember there is also the strange quantum mechanical phenomenon called non-locality. This theory states that once any particle of matter has been in contact with another particle, then when one particle changes it causes a corresponding change in its original partner. This applies wherever in the universe the partner particle ends up. This can be seen to cause a web of interconnectedness which may in some way give a possible path for the energies of thoughts to travel across. Conventional scientists may say that this only happens at sub-atomic level, not to people at all. We do consist of combinations of sub-atomic particles, though, and as an explanation it cannot be dismissed out of hand.

Interestingly enough recent articles in the newspapers and other media indicate that science is beginning to take the phenomenon seriously at last, and is beginning to accept that it actually exists. Its existence is some sort of extra proof of the interconnectedness of things. It almost certainly strengthens the case for the existence and use of the energy matrix.

Remote viewing

Along similar lines to telepathy, there is also the slightly more spooky phenomenon known as remote viewing. This involves using the mind to look remotely in particular geographic locations. Often practised by mystics, it was even taken seriously by the Russian and American intelligence services. Remote viewing was to be used for spying on the enemy (or potential enemy). It was used to discover military installations, find lost operatives or crashed aeroplanes and so on. Gifted psychics would use their powers to try and see what the enemy was doing. They then drew or reported what they had seen. There was both a research and an operational unit. The operational unit trained and employed the personnel, the research unit evaluated and researched the phenomena. It was taken under the military wing in response to the CIA becoming concerned that the Soviets were investing both time and a considerable amount of money on research on that and similar phenomena. The project had many names including Grill Flame and Stargate programme. They had some success,

202 ASPECTS OF REALITY

I understand, especially from some particularly skilled operatives. The programme was apparently dropped after twenty years or so and many millions of dollars, out of probable embarrassment as to its unscientific nature and patchy results. Problems included difficulty in evaluating the correctness of the information. It may just not have been considered cost effective. Some people do claim to be able to remote view even today, but I have never managed it. I am told that it is a skill, in theory, doable by all, but needs a high level of psychic skill and practice.

Prayer

By praying to a god, some people believe that they can alter what will happen in the future. This may be seen as asking an outside force for intervention in earthly events. But this can also be seen as a form of using the human mind to change possible futures. If you believe something will happen, then some people think that this increases the chance of it coming to pass.

Intention

Along similar lines, some people believe that if you make your intentions known to the universe, then it will help you fulfill them. This may be achieved be using outside intervention, choosing from possible multiverse futures, or just knowing what you want and taking the opportunities as they present themselves.

Magic

Magic seems to be a way of making things happen using the power of spells. These are spoken words to attain a certain end, often using symbolic props. They often come from ancient practices or rituals. Magic can be described as a method of purportedly manipulating aspects of reality either by supernatural means or through knowledge of occult laws unknown to us. In using spells, the mind is being used to change reality in some way.

For phenomena like telepathy or remote viewing there is, or may be, a possible scientific explanation of how they work. It could be all possible somehow using the energy matrix around us, or a factor of the quantum field. Only time may tell. For prayer and magic it may be slightly more complicated. If they work as the adherents think they do then that does indicate a reality involving a higher or supernatural power.

Predicting the future

There are several mechanisms or different ways of trying to predict the future using the mind. Some people claim to do it by instinct, clairvoyance, dreams or so-called second sight. Some people claim to do it using only their minds, some people do it using props. These props may include cards or symbols, or even the old-fashioned crystal ball. Many practitioners who do this seem to feel that the use of these types of props only enable a higher power of some sort to indicate via the symbols or cards what the future may hold. This may be in answer to specific questions or in general terms. To begin with, the question has to be asked, does it actually happen in practice? I looked at whether people can actually see into the future, and how they claimed to do it.

Second sight or clairvoyance

Some people just seem to know things about the future. Glimpses of other people's futures as well as their own will just seemingly come into their minds. This is sometimes known as second sight or clairvoyance. Both have been well documented over the years. Some people practise clairvoyance professionally. They can look into someone's future if asked, with varying degrees of accuracy.

Many people of Celtic origin in particular claim to have second sight. We have all heard about the skills in particular of the seventh son of the seventh son. There are even people who claim to predict national disasters by dreaming of them beforehand. We all may know of people who suddenly feel that they should not get into a car, or go on a particular train, and then there turns out to be an accident or disaster. Is this animal instinct or some warning from another dimension or source?

Personal experience of second sight

Although I have not personally been blessed with this gift, I have strong examples of experiences from people closest to me.

Firstly, my own mother had the second sight. She could sometimes see the future. This skill was unasked for and indeed sometimes really frightened her. There was, as far as we know, no history of this ability in her family, and in fact they were very strongly establishment and mainstream. They would have been horrified if they had known, and would almost certainly have not approved at all. That this gift came in those circumstances was amazing. She was then sought out by family and friends to look at their future, but often said no, as sometimes the burden of the information coming to her, from where she knew not, was too disturbing. Personally, she warned me of a completely unexpected personal catastrophe which simply could not have been known about. She was proved right a short time later. She felt she could not see the whole future all the time but, as if clouds were clearing, could suddenly receive glimpses or insights. Unfortunately I have not (as yet anyway) inherited her gifts.

Secondly, something very strange happened when I was being driven along a twisty, narrowish road by my husband. He suddenly sounded his horn at a place that he has not ever done so before. It was just before a bend. The road, however was big enough for two cars to pass with care. We had often driven down that road without difficulty and without ever needing or thinking we should sound a warning. As we rounded the bend this time, another car came driving in the opposite direction at a great speed. It was almost out of control. If we had not alerted him to our presence, an accident may have quite possible occurred. Neither my husband nor myself had heard him approach. Why did Toby then sound his horn at that point, without thinking about it or discussing it? Did he pick up a danger warning from the emotions of a out of control driver? Was it second sight? Was he warned via the energy matrix? Did angelic intervention save us? Was it a higher power or animal instinct? It may have been as simple as his subconscious mind detecting perhaps a change in air pressure or similar which might have indicated something rushing towards us. Whatever it was, it was very useful. It does however show the difficulties in detecting what is explainable in our world, and what is something quite different.

Second sight is hard to quantify. Some people, of course, will just be in possession of a high level of intuition or life experience which will enable them to guess, with impressive accuracy, what the possible outcome of any event would likely be. This just makes them look as if they are seeing the future. There is even a case which says that if you are told of a possible future, you are more likely to make decisions which would make it happening more likely. This is particularly true if you believe that the power of the human mind can override and change possible futures or outcomes.

The interpretation of dreams

Interpretation of dreams is something that is almost a cottage industry. Books are written and even prominent psychiatrists will sometimes analyze your dreams as a clue to what may be going on in your subconscious. Some people do feel that they have prophetic dreams as mentioned earlier. They feel that they can sometimes see the future in their dreams, before it actually happens. I personally know of someone who claims she always dreamt about it when something bad was going to happen to her close friends or family. Is this all coincidence? It has to be considered what the actual purpose of dreams is. Are they just a jumbled insight into the subconscious, or do they sometimes contain information from other sources or higher planes? After all, even our Bible contains stories of dreams and prophecies. Despite much research and speculation over many thousands of years, no one actually can say for sure. They may just be our brains doing nightly housekeeping. They may be a reflection of higher realms. We do not really know.

Divination using props

There are several types of props that people use to help predict the future. These are just a few that have come to my attention:
•   Using a crystal ball. Some clairvoyants claim to be able to see

patterns, shapes or visions to enable them to predict the future.

• Using tea leaves. People have been known to use the patterns made from tea leaves in the bottom of tea cups to see your fate.

• Using ordinary playing cards. Some people, including my late mother, use ordinary playing cards to see the seeker's future. Each card they choose is supposed to have a significance, both in the type of card and its position in the hand. This is supposed to work as a higher power, or even your own subconscious, directs your choice of card. The theory is that focusing on what you need to know will pull in the answers from somewhere, for the reader to interpret. It is worth pointing out that the client's reaction to what has already been said may influence what is then predicted though.

• Using Tarot cards. Along similar lines, there is almost a cottage industry around Tarot card reading. Tarot is a complex and ancient set of symbolic cards. These are packs of 78 cards, these consisting of four sets of 14 cards called minor arcanas and 22 major arcanas. Each card is decorated with symbols, pictures or sometimes numbers. Packs vary in design from traditional to modern.

One theory is that Tarot originally came from Egypt although there are many other legends of its origins. As far as I can tell 'modern' Tarot was developed in France in the 15th century. As with the ordinary playing cards, the practitioner will use their skills to interpret the cards as chosen by the seeker. You will be required to shuffle the cards to put your energy into them, and then they will be laid out in certain formations. These formations vary from practitioner to practitioner. The position or order of the cards is also supposed to determine their significance. The readings are supposed to predict future events or characteristics of those seeking enlightenment. Is it usually accurate? This seems to depend on the skill of the reader. Some are known to be very accurate, above chance. Many people make their living doing readings, especially in places like Glastonbury.

• Using I Ching. This is another major and ancient method of prop-based divination. This consists not of cards but of coins or yarrow sticks and a book which interprets what the sticks or coins have indicated. This is an eastern tradition, although now used all over the world. The tradition involves throwing the coins or sticks and converting the results into numbers. You throw them with a particular question in mind, on the topic on which you are requesting guidance. These numbers are then used to construct a hexagram. The meaning of the particular hexagram can be found in the book of I Ching. This will give you the answer to your question. For instance, a combination of two particular hexagrams will indicate number 62. This is called HSIAO KUO (small things). It says in my version:

"Do not aim too high, the bird's song is sweeter when it is flying low. Small things may be done successfully but not large things. Attend to the small details, especially in public endeavours."

You would then apply this to the question. This particular answer above can be seen as relatively obvious. Do not embark on any large enterprises at the moment. Watch the detail. Often the divinations can be a lot more obscure and can be interpreted in many different ways.

How could divination using props work?

When discussing what could be going on, there seems to be a divide between those people who believe that the practitioners may be pulling from your subconscious information that you already know, but are not conscious of, and those that believe the coins, sticks or tea leaves fall with guidance from a higher power. Also, if you are told what will happen you may subconsciously work towards it happening and make choices which would enable it; for instance, when told that you are going to meet a tall, dark and handsome stranger you actually look out for one, thus creating the future for yourself. Many practitioners who do this seem to feel that the use of these types of props enable a higher power of some sort to indicate via the symbols or cards what the future may hold. But most practitioners, as I understand it, do not necessarily concern themselves about the meaning of the gift or how it can happen, they just know that predicting the future, using their minds and the props, is somehow possible.

The difficult questions

If you believe that second sight and clairvoyance exist and divination with props is possible, then does this mean the future has already happened? Or could it all be pre-planned? If it is pre-planned what does that mean for the nature of creation or being? There are several possibilities:

- It may be that the information is coming from a different dimension.

- It may be that our lives have been planned out in advance and the Tarot, or ordinary cards, or I Ching, or even reading the tea leaves, are just telling us what has been pre-planned to happen.

- The reader could be accessing the Akashic Records, if they exist.

- It may be that the reader is just accessing the subconscious of the seeker and predicting what they would like as a future.

- It may be that deciding on that future enables it to happen.

An alternative view of the future

If the future is not pre-planned, then where could this information about it come from? If you look back to the physics of cosmology, then our future could be seen to be just a possible future of many simultaneous futures (the multiverse). This would then validate the theory that being told that something will happen to you makes it more likely to happen. There are of course also those people who believe that the future can be changed or ordered by prayer, spells or intentions. This is another great hint. How and why could this be possible if it does happen? Well, thoughts are energy; we live in an energy matrix. The answer to this may possibly be seen in quantum mechanics. If you remember, when energy changes form it takes all possible paths instantaneously. It only settles down to one form when someone observes it. Although scientists will say that this only affects the quantum level and not us as individuals, we are fundamentally made of the quantum particles. Could all possible futures be there, and we just choose one by observing or being told that it is the most likely? It is also a possibility that the future is more set than we think and some people with special gifts or sensitivities do get glimpses of what may happen to an individual.

Telepathy and remote viewing could be seen as just picking up information from the bio-energy of thoughts emanating from other people's subconscious minds, using the energy matrix. As mentioned before, until we really understand the true nature of the big picture, these questions are unanswerable. What goes on does hint very strongly at a purposeful, rather than a random, life however.

We cannot, though, see the absolute truths in these matters, just glimpses of these strange reflections of reality. The actual truth of the matter can only be properly determined when we understand the whole of the big picture of our nature and existence. All I can say now is, the phenomena of divination of the future, using the mind to change the future, communicating and viewing with the mind are powerful exceptions to the rules of what should be possible for mere biological beings. Many interesting aspects of reality are indicated.

Aspects of reality

- Thought seems to be able to travel across the energy matrix enabling telepathy.

- The mind seems to be able to travel across the energy matrix to enable remote viewing.

- Therefore our minds are not just contained in our biological bodies

- Some people seem to get glimpses of the future.

- Some people claim to be able to alter the future by prayer. If successful this may indicate the possibility of a higher power. It also may just illustrate the power of the human mind to change the future.

- Some people claim to be able to alter their future by the use of spells and magic. This indicates the possibility of a higher (even occult) power, or just the power of the human mind.

- The mechanism by which some people glimpse the future may indicate that it is pre-planned.

- If seeing the future is possible, does that mean it has already happened?

- There is a possibility that all possible futures exist simultaneously, as in the multiverse.

- Therefore there is a possibility that being told our future makes it more likely to happen.

The most interesting fundamental question generated by these aspects of reality then is that of the nature of the future. Is the future written already? Are we, and could we be, born with our lives pre-programmed? Or could all possible futures exist and we are merely, on some level, choosing between them? If either of these cases are true then what does that say about the aspects of reality concerning our true origins, and the true big picture of life on earth? To help solve this conundrum I then looked at the methods of divination of the future which indicate a universal pre-planning or code.

CHAPTER FIFTEEN

Divination using universal codes

As we can see, the strange skills of telepathy and divination of the future hint at realities beyond those that should be possible if humanity were only earthly biological beings. There is, however, another category of strange ways of predicting the future that show a possible different, even stranger, big picture of reality. There are those methods of divination that seem to tap into some vast universal codes. I include in this things like astronomy, palmistry and numerology. These, if believed accurate at all, would indicate a pre-planning or an order to life which would open up many interesting possibilities concerning the very nature of the human race and a whole new slant on reality.

Astrology

Astrology is the study of the heavens, the sun the moon and planets and the combinations of stars in the night sky, and how they affect the fates of those on earth. It is a very ancient divination tool. The beginnings of astrology are lost in the sands of time, but the discipline is thought to be at least 4,000 years old. It has been considered a serious practice, at least by a certain section of the population for most of that time. It is taken very seriously indeed by many people today. Horoscopes are drawn, usually for individuals, which can be said to explain both their character, their life possibilities and problems for the future.

Horoscopes

A horoscope is actually just a map of the heavens taken at a particular time. It shows where each planet is, and the sun and moon, in relation to the constellations. The constellations are just the groups of stars in the sky that the ancient saw as pictures. They gave them names which we then use to describe our so-called star signs. There are twelve of them, such as Aries the ram and Capricorn the goat. It is these that give us our notional star signs. Many of us are tempted to read the "stars" in our daily newspapers. I myself can never resist it. It is the position of the sun, in whatever constellation happens to be in the sky, at your moment of birth, which is supposed to give you your sign and thus underlying personality. These twelve signs of the zodiac are meant to indicate our character and characteristics. The general horoscopes are offering some prediction of the type of week or month that we may expect for that star sign. As ever it is tempting to interpret what is said to suit your circumstances at the time.

This is obviously general and broad brush. For instance, Capricorns are those born between 22nd of December and 19th of January. I am a Capricorn, therefore along with one twelfth of the population I am supposed to share Capricornian characteristics. Also Capricorn fortune. Part of my predicted character I would actually agree with. I am, or at least try to be, confident, ambitious, strong-willed and generally successful. The other half, cold and distant, stuck in my ways is not me at all. Purists would argue that this is not real astrology at all. It does not take account of the positions of other planets at the time of your birth which might mitigate this.

For instance, my horoscope for the next fortnight ahead, according to the Sunday papers last week, (Catherine Tennant), stated that:

"As yours is the sign that rules the winter solstice, you should be in your element, so take advantage of the opportunities that come your way to live life to the full. Time off from your usual routine is also due to help you find a new way forward. Something you discover on the 27th should give you a winning hand."

This is quite general, probably too general to be of use, but some might find it useful.

Similarly, Scorpio for the same time states that:

"Deepening existing bonds and building firm foundations for the future may be your priorities, but insist that others also give you extra

space. A new relationship has the stars behind it, so back your hunch about someone's feelings. A conversation later in the week gives you an advantage."

Both these statements give very general light guidance only. They could be interpreted to mean many things, depending on the reader.

Patterns in the stars

The funny thing is though, what could be dismissed as nonsense does seem to have more than a grain of truth in it. For instance, if I meet someone new that I am really drawn to the amount of times that they are a fellow Capricorn is above average. I have many friends that either share my birthday or are within a week or so of it. Similarly, I have a lot of friends born mid-May. These are even stranger, as friends and acquaintances born then seem either to be exceptionally kind (above average) or exceptionally selfish (above average). Interesting patterns do seem to be detectable. I am also told that certain professions do seem to clump around certain star signs. According to some theories those born in Aries are more likely to become designers and sales people. Similarly, Cancerians tend to be small traders or teachers or members of the caring professions. This is probably anecdotal evidence only. But it does, from my personal experience, have a ring of truth to it.

Complex astrology

Real astrology is a complex mapping of the heavens at the time of your birth, or at a point in your future. As I understand it, along with the constellations there are the twelve houses, or segments. These include, for instance, home and family, or career, ambition, reputation and honour.

The planets also represent their own particular different aspects or characteristics. These, depending on their position at the time of your birth and when the horoscope is drawn, will affect your future. For instance, Saturn is supposed to be limiting; he may slow down events or make sluggish anything that you may do. This may be especially in any business project. If he was in your sun sign when you were born, or is in your house now, this may affect your plans. There may be counter-balancing planets or heavenly bodies in your chart that may mitigate this influence, or even make things worse, however.

The moon is supposed to show the characteristics of your sub-conscious or, in certain circles it is believed, your soul. The position of the planets, and sun, the moon and also which planet is rising at the moment of your birth all influence who you are. The rising planet, or the Ascendant, is supposed to indicate your temperament, or even according to some, your physical appearance. Also important is your ruling planet. This is the ruler of your Sun sign. There are also many other complex factors to take into account.

Classical astrologers look at the position and interaction of all these elements at the moment of your birth and at subsequent times. For this you need to know the exact time of your birth (GMT) which is often a problem. Even a few minutes may make a difference. This will, in skilled hands, allow them to predict your character; your path of life. For instance, if you have a limiting planet in your house of career this may be a problem. Other planet positions may mitigate this, though. The true process is very complex and relies very much on the individual skills of the practitioner.

Personal research

For research purposes I consulted a professional astrologer to do my own chart. My problem was that I did not know my time of birth. This can cause real problems as it is particularly important to know the position of all the heavenly bodies at your time of birth. Charac-teristics implied by your sun sign can be moderated or mitigated by the position of other bodies at the given time. The so-called ascending sign is vitally important and so is the moon sign. The ascending sign is the one rising on the eastern horizon at the time and place of your birth. For instance, in lots of ways I am a typical Capricorn. The cold side of this sign can be mitigated by various planets in other aspects. Timing therefore is vital.

My astrologer then asked me for important past dates so she could pin down my time of birth for an accurate reading. These I gave her and she was able, by working backwards, to pinpoint my time of birth to 2pm. She then was able to give me a more accurate horoscope. As it happens, at this birth time, my ascendant is in Gemini and my moon is in Taurus.

According to some interpretations at least, my Capricorn sun sign will make me strong, practical, ambitious and reserved. I am certainly the former but not the latter. It will also, on the negative side, make me pessimistic, fatalistic, and grudging. These I am most definitely not. These are mitigated by the moon in Taurus which gives me my good instincts and an affectionate romantic nature. My Gemini ascendant gives me my questioning and curious nature (also possibly my alleged quirky side!). It is not as simple as that in practice because all the other planets have an influence. Do we choose our time of birth according to what life we want to live? It is an intriguing thought.

Variations on a theme

There are also many variations on what we consider classic astrology. There are many different ways of mapping and interpreting the heavens to the same end. It may vary with individual culture and handed down traditions. For instance, the Chinese have a different system. It is based on the cycles of the moon not the sun. There are twelve named animals such as rat and tiger. Each has its own characteristics. For instance Tigers are born leaders. The year then has the characteristics of the animal, not just the person born in them. For instance, Dragon years may be unusually creative. The end result is a melding of all the factors by skilled practitioners to create a personal or group horoscope.

It is, I am told, often used to determine the best or most auspicious time for starting projects or entering into contracts, including marriage. It is not unusual for those entering into marriage to compare personal horoscopes to ascertain long term compatibility as well as the best time for the wedding to occur. My husband and I are very compatible although we come from different backgrounds. In the Chinese astrology it becomes clear why. He is a Tiger (Grrrh) and

I am an Ox. Tigers may be too much for most animals, but I am an ox, therefore tigers do not worry me.

Does Astrology work?

Well, in skilled hands there does seem to be something there. There are many people who make their living out of it. It seems, by all accounts, to rely on the skill and intuition of the reader to make sense of the many affecting factors. It is taken very seriously by some cultures and in some circles of our own. Queen Elizabeth I had her own court Astrologer, Dr John Dee. He was frequently consulted before decisions were made. Most astrologers seem to say they are predicting trends rather than absolutes. This means possible success, possible problems or dangers. Projecting the planetary paths into the future and looking at the possibilities indicated by their position may not be quite the same as giving possible 'hard' future predictions. If Mars is in a certain position or conjunction, then a war or conflict is more likely but not inevitable. You could be told that you may have a likely bad day on a certain date, to beware of potentially dangerous situations. It does not seem possible to predict purely using Astrology, that you were going to trip over walking, break your right leg and that the hospital where it would be set was going to be flooded, and your husband would run off with your neighbour whilst you were out and so on. Most astrologers say that it should be used as a guidance system.

Possible mechanism for the working of astrology

The interesting thing though, is why, if it does work, even on the level of generalisations and trends, could this be possible? What mechanism or explanation could there be for such a phenomenon? How could this fit into a possible big picture of the universe? What aspect of reality does this reveal ? How could it possibly work?

One theory is that as we are beings made of vibrating pulses of energy and the planets and stellar bodies emit energy themselves, this affects our brain structure at the time of our birth. The sun, being the most powerful, affects everyone born about the same time the same way. Thus our sun signs (e.g. Virgo, Taurus, etc) could indicate similarities in characteristics. We are well aware of how the moon affects humanity. Tides we all know, but also the moon affects thing such as biorhythms, menstrual cycles and even the best time to plant or harvest crops. Lunatics (mad men) are also known to be adversely affected at certain stages of the moon.

The ancient view

Surprisingly, an understanding of this mechanism was given in the 16th Century. Dr John Dee, the famous Tudor court astrologer of the time, theorised that the rays emitting from the heavenly bodies affected the soul as well as the body. (*The Queen's Conjuror* by Benjamin Woolly). We, after all, are living in and are part of the energy matrix as previously described. The planets and heavenly bodies are part of that matrix and so there may be a possible logical and scientific pathway for it to work.

Modern understanding

Jonathan Cainer, the famous Astrologer, explains the mechanism wonderfully. When asked how astrology could possibly predict human behavior he stated that:

"It can be comprehended if you understand that all things are composed of the same energy but vibrating at different rates. It also helps if you think of our solar system as one being, similar to an atom which has neutrons and protons orbiting a central nucleus."

If you were high enough, you could look down on our solar system as it travels though the universe and see it as an immensely vast series of unbelievably intricate patterns of energy all linked and interacting with each other. So in the same way that ripples are created on the surface of water by a stone being dropped into it, the energy of the full moon pulls babies out of the womb (ask any midwife when is her busiest time) and creates trouble after closing time outside the pub (ask any policeman).

The role of astrology

Astrology can be seen as some sort of cosmic Satellite Navigation system (Satnav). The theory is that the role of an astrologer is to inform you of the nature of the planetary energies that are influencing your life at any given time. This knowledge then enables you to steer your life in the desired direction using the prevailing cosmic winds as your allies, rather than struggling against them through lack of awareness.

The purpose of astrology may be to give guidance though life. Like a satnav, it can show you the best path and guide you past the obvious dangers and pitfalls. If you read it right it can make life easier and indicate the best time to do things. If you deviate from the right path, it can recalculate to the next best options. As a bonus it can explain why things are not going smoothly (planets in the wrong quadrant) but that it is not personal, but will pass. It can even explain why friends and colleagues are acting a certain way, and allow you not to take it personally.

Grand plan?

The unanswerable question though is why the universe is set up this way? If Astrology is in any way valid what does this say about the big picture? Does it indicate the work of a grand planner, and astrology just helps us interpret the plan? Does it show that the perception of the universe as just a gigantic mathematical model is the most valid? Or are these emanations that affect our lives just a by-product of the way the universe has naturally or randomly evolved? Some people who believe it is all planned also think that you choose your date and time of birth to live the life that you want. If you have a life's mission you choose the time that will maximize your chance of succeeding. Is this likely? We cannot really begin to even try to answer any of that until we have more accurately looked through these reflections to the true nature of reality itself. This is probably both beyond our capability and not meant to be.

Palmistry

There is another popular phenomenon, that if valid, may indicate a pre-planning of life. I refer to palmistry. This can also be known as Chiromancy and is another ancient and much-practised skill. The image of a gypsy giving accurate future predictions by looking at your hand is somewhat misleading, though there may be some that can do that using some level of psychic skills as well as looking at your palm. The palm itself, my researches have led me to understand, is more an indication of character and traits. These traits are allegedly laid down by your genetic code before birth. It is, in practice, more another satnav tool than a hard future predictor. Some do say, however, that it is also affected by your soul and it is possible, with skill, to use palmistry to foretell the future. Today, however, this does seem to be the minority position. Most palmists I have spoken to use it to do character analysis only. By looking at the character and health clues in your palm, then with knowledge of your position, hopes and dreams, a generalized future can be projected forward somewhat. This is not the same as seeing a 'hard' future in your hands.

Could your future be imprinted on your hands before birth? Can your health be indicated by palm size, finger length and colour of nails and skin? Well on one level that is not far-fetched. Things like comparative finger length has recently been proved to be an indicator of testosterone levels in the womb. Nail shape has long been thought an indicator of heart problems. Circulation problems can be detected in the colour of the skin on the hands. Other genetic markers like this may also exist in the lines and bumps in the hand. Some do even say that homosexuality is inherited and can be shown in a certain V-shaped line on the hand.

The mechanics of palmistry

Where palmistry rises above current science is in the more esoteric readings of the lines and bumps. On reading your hand, most practitioners will look at the lines, ridges and shapes and their interaction. For instance, according to some practitioners, a straight heart line means that the head tends to rule the heart. A 'V' above this line may denote empathic qualities. As with astrology, the meaning of different lines and bumps cannot be read in isolation. Their interaction is just as important. For instance, lines showing the tendency to be a free spirit may be modified by stiffish thumbs (which could indicate a tendency towards rigidity).

The theory is that your dominant hand, usually your right hand, has marks that will change over the years. The other hand is your destiny hand and this has your intended fate in it and will stay the same over your lifetime. I am told that it is not as simple as that in practice, but those are the general principles with which most people work.

Satnav or fixed fates?

It does seem that you can override what is written on your hands at birth. The indications of possible paths in life, and the characteristics which may enable you to achieve them, may be there at birth. However, free will may override and change the lines on your dominant hand. For instance, when I consulted a practitioner, I was told that my dominant hand showed more spiritual development and creativity than my passive hand showed to be my fate.

Palmistry then can be used as an indicator of health and as a satnav of guidance, using the revealed traits to help plan an effective future. Some practitioners, of course, will use other psychic skills to look into your personal future. This brings us back to the really interesting question here, though: if you believe that your fate is written in your hand at birth, does it mean that life is pre-planned?

Numerology and other codes

There is another set of disciplines which also strongly suggests a pre-planning of life in some form. One of the main ones is numerology. This can be seen as an offshoot of another ancient skill which goes back at least to the time of the Greek philosophers. This involves the premise that numbers are sacred and significant. Pythagoras, the mathematician, felt that number was the basis of all things. Numbers have meanings of their own. By manipulating them, cracking the code, we can find our life's purpose. Spiritual laws exist and govern the structure and forces of the universe and our lives. By breaking the codes encrypted in these numbers we can find our own life path. These theories have come down to us via the Greeks, Egyptians and the ancient Kabbalists, as well as many others, all seeking to crack the code of life. Modern numerology, the system used today by most practitioners, seems to have been developed by the same famous late sixteenth century scholar, mentioned earlier, Dr John Dee. He is considered one of the founding fathers. He was working on many projects, including the occult sciences and astrology.

The mechanics of numerology

The theory of numerology is that our names and date of birth are significant. By converting the letters of our names into numbers we can uncover our character, heart and personality. This is done using a code. Every letter has a number assigned to it, from one to nine. To find out about ourselves (at least in the system I looked at) the resulting numbers are added up. If it is ten or over then these figures are also then added together. For example 13 would become $1 + 3$ which would equal 4. Adding up the vowels only would give heart character, adding up consonants gives personality. If my name added up to a 7 then the book says this means that I am a natural loner, a recluse, someone who enjoys solitude and working alone. A total of 8 indicates a practical and dogged nature.

Whether you believe in the principle or not there are many obvious problems with name analysis. Personally I have never used my legal first name. My parents realised they had made a naming mistake soon after my birth, as my birth name was similar to my mother's name and caused confusion. I have always been known by my second name. Also, I have been married three times so have had four surnames, including my maiden name. I have, therefore, had eight possible combinations of name, depending if you use my official first name or the one I am always known by. If I use both Christian names that actually gives me twelve variations. Adding up these different combinations gives me different values. Which numbers or names do I actually use?

Personal sums

There are two possible answers to this question. Firstly, I am told that you must use the name that you are most usually known by. This then eliminates four of my possibilities. The surname used could be my maiden name. Second name and maiden name then give me a character number of 2. Reading the explanation I am certainly not, or never have been a 2. Using my official first name gives me a 1. This is much more me. So my real birth name may be significant. Using both names and my surname, I am a 3. I can see traits of a 3 about me. So when I was born, according to numerology theory, my real name and my full name gave me my character. It was not relevant that I was called by my middle name. The name I was supposed to be called was important.

What about my different married names? Funnily enough the values of my current and last married names, both add up to a 1. My first married name is again a 3. These values could be manipulated to give different results time and time again. The interesting thing is, quite unexpectedly, that a pattern does emerge quite strongly. Time and time again 1 and 3 came up. Both of these do chime in with a lot that I know to be my character.

Multiple codes

There is, however, a second major problem with numerology. This is which number code do you use? Who is to say which is the correct one? There are slightly different numbering systems according to whether you feel drawn to the Hebrew or Latin convention. Who is to say why certain letters have certain values whatever numbering system is used?

Life path prediction

There is another interesting aspect of numerology which, rather than describing character, actually predicts life path. This is, as in astrology, worked out on your date of birth. In this you just add up the numbers in a straight forward manner. My date of birth was:

$$31.12.1949 - 31+12+1949 = 1992 - 1+9+9+2=21$$

This again makes me a three. Others recommend adding every digit separately. This gives me 30 which is still a 3 (3+0=3). The 1 of my name and the 3 of my birth date actually harmonize. I can see aspects of my character in both. If they were the same it would emphasize the characteristics. I am told that if the given characteristics conflicted then there would always be some inner conflict in your character. I am told then numerologically that I am a 30/3. This number will therefore show me, in theory, my life path. Can this be possible? Also, by adding day and month of birth to any year, it is thought possible to determine the characteristics of every year on a nine year cycle. It would be possible to determine in theory what sort of year that you were going to have. As a 30/3 I am told that I came into this world with a strong creative energy and drive. This does fit the bill with my writing and communicating skills. It is nice to think that I may be fulfilling my life's purpose in writing this book!

Before embarking on my research, numerology seemed to me to be the strangest and least logical of all the tools of divination. How could it, given the problems as outlined above, actually work? I was very surprised at the personal patterns that emerged. It does not, along with any of the other disciplines that I have looked at such as astrology and palmistry, seek to tell your hard future. It is, in the end, just another type of satnav indicational tool. The interesting thing is though, that it does on some level seem to work, and the mystery is how this could be possible. Unless of course these numbers are somehow embedded in us and our reality in a way beyond our current understanding.

Big picture questions

The other big picture questions that astrology and numerology and their like pose are even stranger. If they truly work, then this calls into question the very meaning of life itself. Do we, could we, really choose our date and time of birth? Are our given names significant? Could any of these factors actually influence our life paths and what will happen to us? What explanations are possible? What big picture of creation could this be a reflection of?

There may of course be some practical explanations. Could this be just nature's way of randomising life, to give greater diversity and thus maximise survival of the species? Are these patterns just a natural property of living in the energy matrix? Are the practitioners just tapping in to natural laws that are not properly or generally understood? Or do we, at a higher level get to choose the sort of life we need to experience? If it is the latter, from what level or plane of existence do we make this decision? What does it say about the true nature both of the universe in particular and reality in general? We are back to the difficult and fundamental, and probably unanswerable, questions.

The universal, mechanical or spiritual laws that these skills seek to interpret and that seem to be encoded in the movements of the planets or in the letters and numbers of our existence, may yet turn out to be scientifically explainable. This will happen only when the real big picture of how the universe operates has been understood. Whether this will turn out to be purely written by the random mechanical nature of the universe or by an intelligent designer of some sort will be interesting to see.

Aspects of reality

- There seem to be satnav type systems of guidance in place in the universe for humanity, in the form of Astrology and Numerology.

- The study of Palmistry may indicate that guiding information may be encoded in the palms of our hands.

- This may indicate that a grand plan may exist somewhere.

- There may exist a planner who is putting in place this guidance.

- It may indicate that the universe is a gigantic mathematical model.

All of this does indicate that the big picture of life is more complex than those that believe in just a random Darwinian existence would allow. We cannot, though, see the absolute truths in these matters, just glimpses of strange reflections. What realities these reflections might indicate though, is the last great mystery.

CHAPTER SIXTEEN

Seven Aspects of Reality

In this, my personal journey towards trying to understand the nature of the reality in which humanity finds itself living, I have looked at all the many and various clues which were within my reach. In any search for ultimate truths we can only rely on the evidence available. I refer you again to the study of reality being akin to looking at the reflections from an old fashioned glitter-ball suspended from the ceiling. As the ball turns and turns above our heads, all we can see are the reflections. Some reflections may be distorted by the light. Some reflections may even seem to contradict each other due to our incomplete grasp of the big picture.

The glimpses into possible realities given to us by many topics, especially the things that should not be possible if we were *only* biological beings, hint at different big pictures than those taught by mainstream society. Science and religion both have their views of course, but whatever they say no one can say for certain what the ultimate nature of reality actually is. It has to be remembered that humanity's grasp of our physical reality is wrong from the start. We are not standing still on a solid planet as we perceive ourselves to be; we are actually rushing though space on a rotating disc. What else could we be totally wrong about?

The more I looked at all these aspects of reality the more difficult it all became. The reflections of reality seemed more confused, not clearer. I found fewer concrete answers than I would have hoped for, only more and more questions. Even a glimpse of the possible implications of quantum theory, multiverse and holographic theory, raises strange possibilities for the nature of reality. Could we really be fixing what is around us by just observing? Is our personal reality all in our mind? Are we even just an interactive video game. Can we switch dimensions or universes at will, are we just reflections of a reality elsewhere? What do we actually know for sure about the actual nature of the reality that we find ourselves living in?

Seven aspects of reality

I gathered together all the reflections of reality that I had looked at and identified seven main strands. There may be others that have not yet been identified. Some reflections seem to contradict each other, some get jumbled up, some are strong, some are weak, but the following are what I have been able to perceive and come to understand. They are what is available to us as mere human beings.

First aspect of reality

What actually are we ? Although we think we are solid biological beings, our atomic structure shows us that we are are at base nothing more than beings made of vibrating pockets of energy. We can be seen to be living in in an energy matrix. Even our thoughts are nothing more than bio-energy. Some people can communicate tele-pathically with others, using this energy matrix. Science does not yet wholly know why the energy from which we and the universe are made acquires mass (solidity). There is also a growing realisation, taken seriously in some scientific circles, that we and the universe may be nothing more than holograms. This does beg the question of where and what the originals might be though.

Second aspect of reality

Where did we come from? There are many creation theories, some more plausible than others. Mainstream science cosmology tells us that creation began with the energy from the Big Bang, which then formed the matter of our universe. It is, though, a total mystery as to where the Big Bang energy came from. As we continue to look further and further back into space and time, so the more questions and anomalies seem to be generated.

Who made us? Are we just random products of chance evolution, or were we created by someone or something? If so it may have been by our traditional creator god, or another type of intelligent designer, or even aliens. The truth may be something completely different of course, beyond our current understanding.

There is so far no proper explanation as to why a random cocktail of chemicals became life. If we were created and given life or seeded, then why? For what purpose?

Third aspect of reality

The reality of the soul. We are not just biological beings. We have a consciousness, or an essence, which some would call a soul. This can be shown to exist alongside our physical animal bodies and the computer-like functions of our genetically determined brain.

This consciousness can be shown to go on after physical death. We can be seen to have multiple lives, as this soul reincarnates in different physical bodies through time. The dead can communicate with the living, often via mediums. Traces of the physically dead, that have not passed to where they should go, can sometimes be seen as ghosts.

Fourth aspect of reality

Science and reality. We live in a multi-dimensional universe, or even multiverse. String theory and Brane theory indicate many interesting possibilities for the nature of reality. There is also the theory that the universe can be seen as nothing more than a series of mathematical equations. It is nothing but a giant mathematical model.

Quantum mechanics gives insight into the fundamental instability, yet interlinkedness, of all matter. The mind seemingly has a role in fixing reality. Reality may be more personal to us than we realise.

Could it actually be possible to be conscious in multiple realities? Could it be possible to change reality? Could we possibly be just choosing, with our consciousness, from the super-state of reality, as per quantum mechanics?

Some people do think that they can change future reality with their minds. They do this with prayer or spells or so-called intention. This can be seen as either invoking higher powers or using your conscious mind to change your possible futures.

Fifth aspect of reality

Multi-layered humanity, Alongside our physical bodies we have a many layered spirit body. This subtle body works alongside our physical body to maintain its health and integrity. This can be re-balanced by practitioners to allow healing. The energy body is powered via the chakras and connected to the universal energy field by the hara. Some people go further and maintain that we grow and develop to a pre-determined blueprint. What sort of big picture would this indicate? Some people claim to be able to leave their physical bodies and astrally travel. None of this should be possible in a world that has not got a spirit dimension.

Sixth Aspect of reality

Planned existence. There are some strange skills that people possess which should not happen if the world was as we were taught it to be. Some people are able to predict the future. Does this mean that the future is pre-planned or has already happened? Is there a giant supercomputer out there somewhere with all of humanity and their many lives pre-programmed? What about the Akashic records? What about karma?

Seventh aspect of reality

We are not alone. Within our reality there are other beings, seem-ingly helping us. There are angels looking after us, and nature spirits helping the plant life of the biosphere. Some people also believe that every rock, building and everything on the earth has its own spirit. The earth itself, Gaia, may even be a sentient being.

Aliens may interact with us. Some people believe that they have interfered with the human genome in the past. This has developed our minds beyond that which normal evolutionary forces would allow.

The search for ultimate truth

These different aspects of reality are sometimes just different ways of looking at the same truths. How can we know which is right and which is just a distorted reflection? The truth is sometimes there but is hidden and confused by misunderstood information. There is probably much there that is fundamental but that we do not, or cannot, see at all.

We are after all limited beings, limited by the quality and nature of our sense organs and the ability of our brains to interpret information. The truth is also overlaid by cultural convention and interpretation of the societies that we live in. The evidence is that we live in a multi-dimensional universe. The nature of these dimensions is not clear, but they are actually a scientific fact. We are energy beings living in an energy matrix. All we can personally count on is the reality generated by our individual consciousness. The fact that our consciousness goes on after physical death in some form is certain. This life is not all there is. The grand big picture, beyond that which we can understand, is to us fundamentally unknowable. Sometimes, even now, the truth looks different to different people, depending on where they are standing under the glitter ball, and where the light is shining at any particular time.

Final thoughts

In any personal journey to truth and understanding, the difficult bit is where to end. There is always more!

There is a big picture out there that begins to emerge, if you look carefully beyond the reflections of reality that we are capable of seeing. What can I say that I have learnt for sure? I can say, almost certainly, is that life is not random accident. Personally I feel that the evidence is almost overwhelming for a soul, a designer, and to some extent a pre-planned life. Also, I feel that the nature of our consciousness, or soul, is somehow a bigger clue than we realize to the puzzle of the true nature (if there is such a thing) of reality. If we truly understood it, then we could follow the reflection back to the ultimate truth. This, however, is not yet possible, and may never be in this lifetime. What can we do with the information we do have, though?

A user's guide to the universe

The final question is then, how can the information, insights and wisdom I have accumulated on my journey through the aspects of our reality be used? There is some sense to be made out of what we can glean from the reflections of reality that we can begin to see. We can use some of these possible truths and understandings to enhance our lives.

•   We do not just vanish at physical death. As we do go on in some form, we must assume that what we do in this life matters. We must live the best lives we can. We may regret it later if we do not. We must be the best people we are capable of being. That will reward us in this life, whatever the form of the next.

•   We will have many lives to do what we want to do. Some lives will be easy, some difficult, some rich, some poor. All are learning and growing experiences; embrace your current life with as much good grace as you can muster.

•   As we may be reincarnated in any position in life, always treat others with respect and understanding. Next lifetime you may find yourself in the situation of the person you have despised or sneered at. Look after those less fortunate than yourselves – you may be in the same position as them next life. Sexual or racial discrimination is therefore absurd.

•   Our genetics may predispose us to act in certain ways. We may or may not be able to able to override them with our soul energy; or may not be aware that we can. Understand that other people may be victims of their genetics and be tolerant of others.

•   We know when we have behaved badly or inappropriately. The result of these actions on our quality of life, and on those others involved with us, will almost certainly be negative. Resolution or at least forgiveness on an inner level will help to counteract this.

• I also feel that, long term, good behaviour tends to be rewarded and bad behaviour punished in this world. Those acting selfishly may appear to get away with it short term, but long term they never do. Act well and you are rewarded with an inner strength and contentment and respect and love of others which makes life worthwhile, whatever your circumstances.

• However flawed some religions may seem to be, there are lessons at their core on how to live life well. These can be very useful guidance. Look at the unselfishness, charity and honour and respect for one another and the earth, that most preach. Use these lessons.

• In a multiple life big picture, the concept of karma explains a lot of seeming unfairness. What goes around comes around. If we understand that when bad things happen to us, we may be just repaying a karmic debt, then it all becomes much easier to deal with.

• All we can be sure about in this seemingly physical world around us, is actually our own consciousness. Whatever the true nature of reality, remember it may be only in our minds.

• Our consciousness is more powerful than most people believe it to be. Our thoughts may be capable of even altering the physical reality around us. If we know what life we want, and what reality we prefer and we send the message out to the universe, we are more likely to achieve it. This is notwithstanding that you cannot and should not interfere with anyone else's free will. Think positive thoughts as much as possible!

• Within that consciousness is our capacity to love each other. Lust is an animal instinct. It is useful to bind people together, to create quick connections. The problem arises when people confuse lust with the deep love that we are all capable of; that is the love that nourishes both ourselves and others and sometimes even puts their interests before our own. We feel this love for partners, family and sometimes friends. This is the real deal. Find it and hang on to it.

•   We should not be distracted by the surface appearance of people, or worry too much about our own appearance. Good looks fade, good character is for ever. Those who obsess with looks are always on to a loser. Fashion will come and go. Our media have a lot to answer for. They perpetuate the myth that fashion and looks and thinness really matter. What should be a bit of fun causes much unhappiness among the gullible and insecure of this world.

•   Material goods really do not matter. Just remember that, despite appearances, more money does not buy more happiness; as long as we have enough to live, of course. Absolute poverty and starvation are unacceptable by any standards. Those that are locked in the consumer rat race can never win. Any esteem just conferred by owning things, is fundamentally unsound. If people judge us by what we own, or what we look like, then they are to be pitied.

•   Life, and we, are worth much more than that. Consumerism never seems to bring solid continuing happiness. It is a race that never stops and can never be won. It is in fact a distraction from what really matters in life.

•   What really matters is what sort of person we are, not what we wear or what we own – that way long term unhappiness and discontent are more likely. This is especially true if we are surrounded by those who judge us solely by those criteria. We must choose our friends well. Remember what really matters in life and do not be distracted by surface shallowness and tat. And of course, we cannot take material goods with us when we die....

•   Human life is difficult but we do get help. Beings from other realms do help and communicate with us. Angels, nature spirits and those dear departed souls known to us, are often there to help us if we choose to listen. We can use the angels and other spirits to enhance our lives and spirituality if we are able. Real happiness is found in the spiritual and not the material world. I ask the angels every day for help and say thank you for that help every evening. I have felt real help, comfort and guidance from these sources through some of the most difficult times in my life. We must talk to and respect the nature spirits to help us live in harmony with the environment and the world.

• Whatever aspect of reality they reflect, do not forget to use the the 'satnavs' that seem to be built into our universe to help us. Astrology, numerology, i ching, runes and other methods can be used for guidance if needed.

Finally, it is always important for us live in the now and enjoy every day. Life is precious. Do not think or say, we will be happy when we are richer, thinner, more famous et cetera. Take pleasure in small things. Always, at the same time, bear in mind the big picture. People get stuck in sadness or misery at small disappointments. It is best to put all joy and sorrow and frustration into proportion and context. We are responsible for what we allow into our conscious minds. We must take responsibility for this. If we can look at the big picture, it almost always helps. Understand that in later life you may well be laughing at things which seemed the end of the world today. Life is to be enjoyed. Sometimes awful things do happen, which actually bring long term changes for the best. You cannot make an omelette without breaking eggs!

Conclusion

We cannot know the actual nature of reality around us. We cannot wholly solve the conundrum of the nature of human life, or complete our puzzle of the true nature of the universe in which we find ourselves existing. What the true big picture is above the dimension in which we can see and in which we exist, is impossible to know. We can just look at the aspects of reality that we can see reflected back into our existence. We can just know that we are not purely biological beings; we have a purpose to our lives. Whatever that true purpose is we cannot really know either. We are born with a blank slate. All we can do is live, act the best we can and enjoy each life to the maximum.

How to end, that is the difficult bit. I have learned so much in my journey. I have come across concepts that are too weird to put down on paper, without looking foolish, yet may well be true. There is more searching, research and exploration to do. Science moves on, cosmology moves on. It has been a long and exhausting journey, but if this has helped anyone to understand and navigate through life better and happier, it has all been worthwhile. Look beyond the surface of the material world, and find truth for yourselves.